D1452328

smart

small car, big deal

This edition published in 2008 by Motorbooks, an imprint of MBI Publishing Company, 400 First Avenue North, Suite 300, Minneapolis, MN 55401 USA

Originally published as smartism © 2007 by Motorbuch Verlag, Postfach 103743, 70032 Stuttgart.

A division of Paul Pietsch-Verlage GmbH & Co.

Produced with the friendly support of smart GmbH and DaimlerChrysler AG

Text contributions by Jürgen Zöllter and Willi Diez

Design and concept: Wolfgang Seidl

Layout, design and realization: SEIDLDESIGN

Cover Design: SEIDLDESIGN, using an image by Gaukler Studios

Editorial Support: Heinz Gottwick, Bernhard Joseph, Hari Ehinger

Photos: DaimlerChrysler image archives, smart GmbH Marketing and Press Department image archives, Gaukler Studios, Sabine Biedermann (Milano), Smartclubs, TrikeTec

English translation: Peter L. Albrecht

Motorbooks titles are also available at discounts in bulk quantity for industrial or sales-promotional use. For details write to Special Sales Manager at MBI Publishing Company, 400 First Avenue North, Suite 300, Minneapolis, MN 55401 USA.

To find out more about our books, join us online at www.motorbooks.com.

ISBN-13: 978-0-7603-3521-5

Printed in Singapore

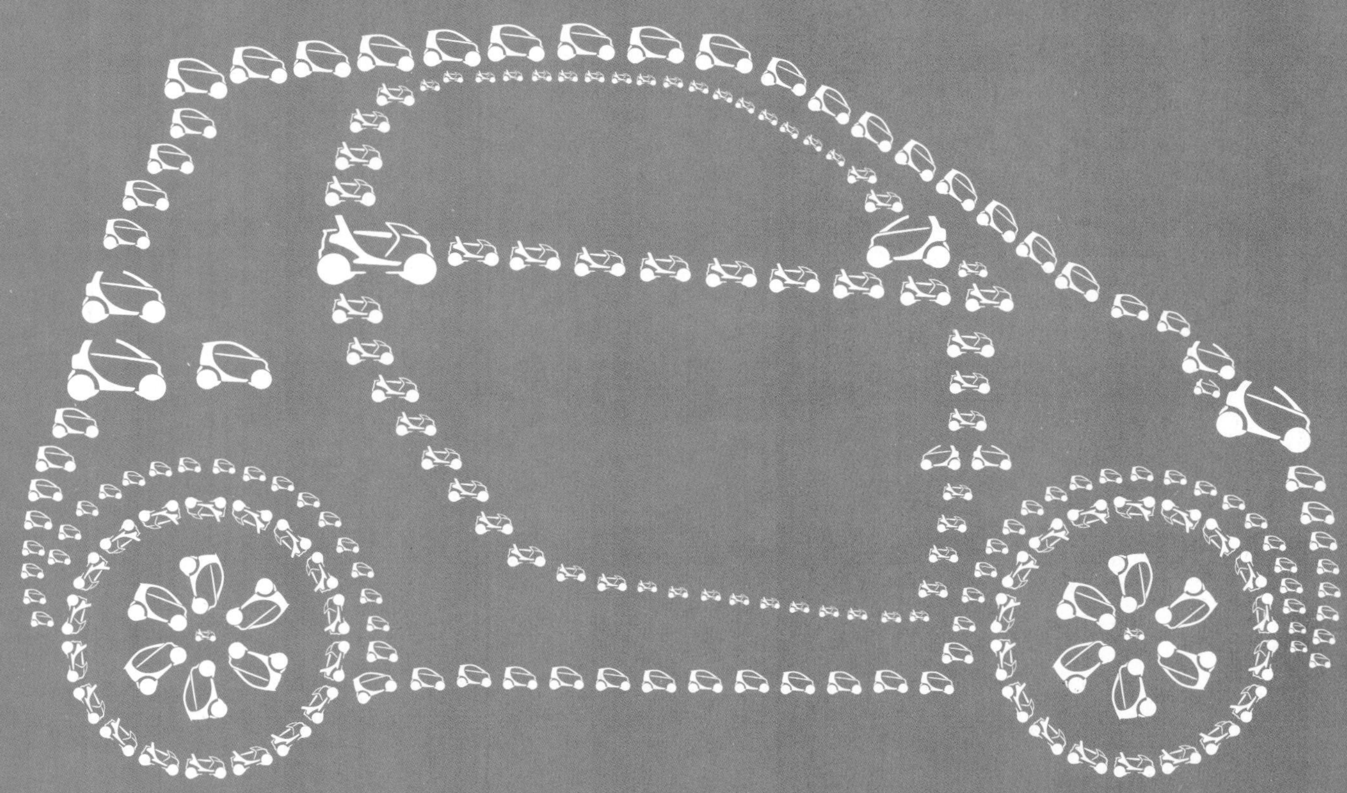

FOREWORD

The smart story is one of **entrepreneurial vision** and a matching portion of **daring.** It is simultaneously a story of German and European innovation, and proof that to be successful, even the best ideas must be appropriate for their time. At Daimler, the roots of an **automotive concept designed specifically for urban use** reaches back to the early 1970s. The growing problems of inner-city individual transportation, a parking situation which was becoming ever more critical even then, and increased **environmental awareness** spurred by the oil crises of the early 1970s and 1980s, helped the smart to its breakthrough in the early 1990s.

The Micro Compact Car Project broke with several long-standing automotive industry

traditions: a revolutionary vehicle concept, new relationships with original equipment suppliers, an innovative production system, and radical new distribution channels. Not all of these were immediately successful; several parameters needed fine tuning. But the result was a completely **new vehicle class**, and a **life-affirming, classless automobile** that offers an answer to many of the questions of our automotive future – and once again makes driving in city traffic an unencumbered experience. In many markets, its users have transformed the smart into a modern-day icon.

A total of 770,000 customers have purchased the first-generation smart fortwo. And, for many, it has become a part of their **individual world views.**

The **streets of Rome are home to 50,000 smarts.** Now, the second generation is coming to market – somewhat more mature, some might say more conventional. But this is especially so because we have gotten accustomed to the smart. As in Rome, it has become part of the city scene in many metropolises, and we have learned to appreciate its virtues.

The second-generation smart remains a typical smart in every respect. But it does everything just a little bit better than its predecessor. It offers its passengers more **comfort**, more **agility**, more **safety** and even more **environmental responsibility.** And, at a time when global warming, carbon dioxide emissions, and miles per gallon are the topics of the day, the smart is the absolute champion for low CO_2 emissions, and therefore more up-to-date than ever. **Authors Willi Diez** and **Jürgen Zöllter** have examined the still recent history of the smart from various perspectives, and related its story as a contemporary chronicle. The result is a **multidimensional image of the marque and the automobile,** an exciting outline of what it means to establish a new automobile brand in our time, and a book which, for the first time, reveals a wealth of previously unreleased material from the history of the smart marque.

Anders Sundt Jensen
Head of smart Brand Team, Global Marketing & Sales

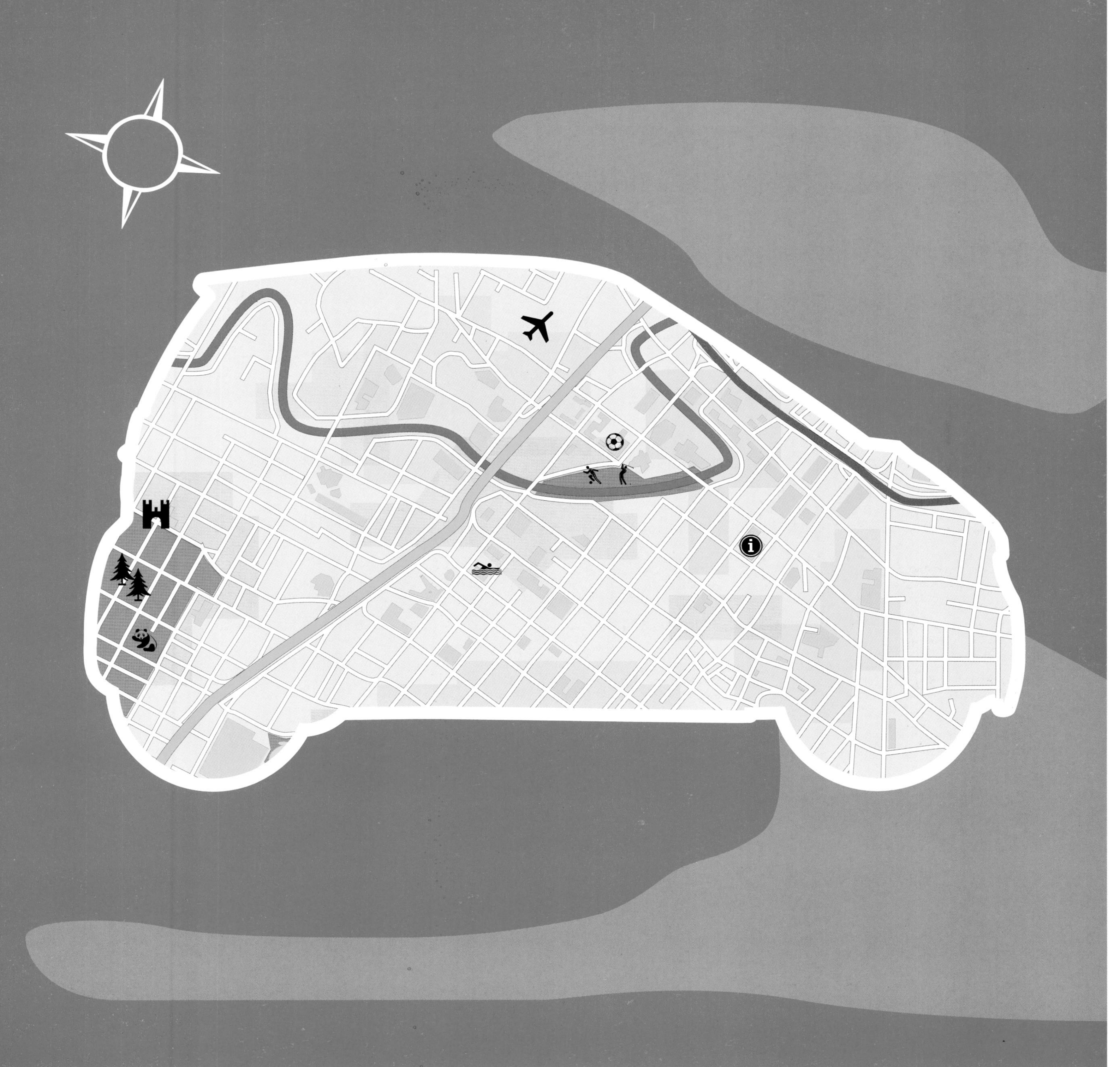

NEW
YO
RK

ONE WAY

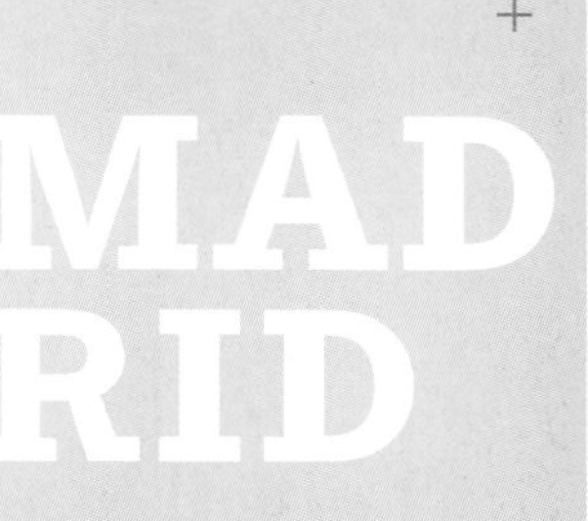
MAD
RID

BER
LIN

LON
DON

MON
TECA
RLO

STO
CKH
OLM

Multilayered: 70% of human body heat is apparently lost from the head – not an especially **efficient system**. Twelve percent of worldwide CO_2 emissions escape through automotive exhaust pipes. In this department, the smart is so efficient that it has been crowned the **CO_2 champion.**

A smart erases class distinctions. Not only that, but **the most beautiful women drive a smart!**

VIETATO
FUMARE
Nesquik
nutella
nutella
MIKADO
Kinder
Happy Hippo
J&B
JAMESON
MOLINARI
STOCK
CREMA CACAO
ROMANA SAMBUCA
PALLINI
MISTRA
DE CECCO
BATIDA DE COCO
WILD TURKEY
LUXARDO
PANEANGELI
Fecola di Patate
PANEANGELI
caffè

Narrow lanes, and especially Roman traffic conditions, demand a **highly maneuverable, agile vehicle.** The best choices are a motor scooter – or a smart.

It makes more sense to spend one's **money for books, organic food, or,** above all, **shoes.** No car should incur any more expense than a smart.

A smart makes life simpler. And **sexy.** For, after all, **modern** is that which satisfies our demands while maintaining **environ-mental responsibility** and practicality. Just like a smart.

Böcker / DVD

FAUNIA
Madrid VISION

SIGHTSEEING

КАФЕ

Lisa Elmqvist
ÖSTERSSON

perie des Canettes

СТОП
IAN FRUIT

ЛЕТНИЙ
ОБЕД
TODO
A 100

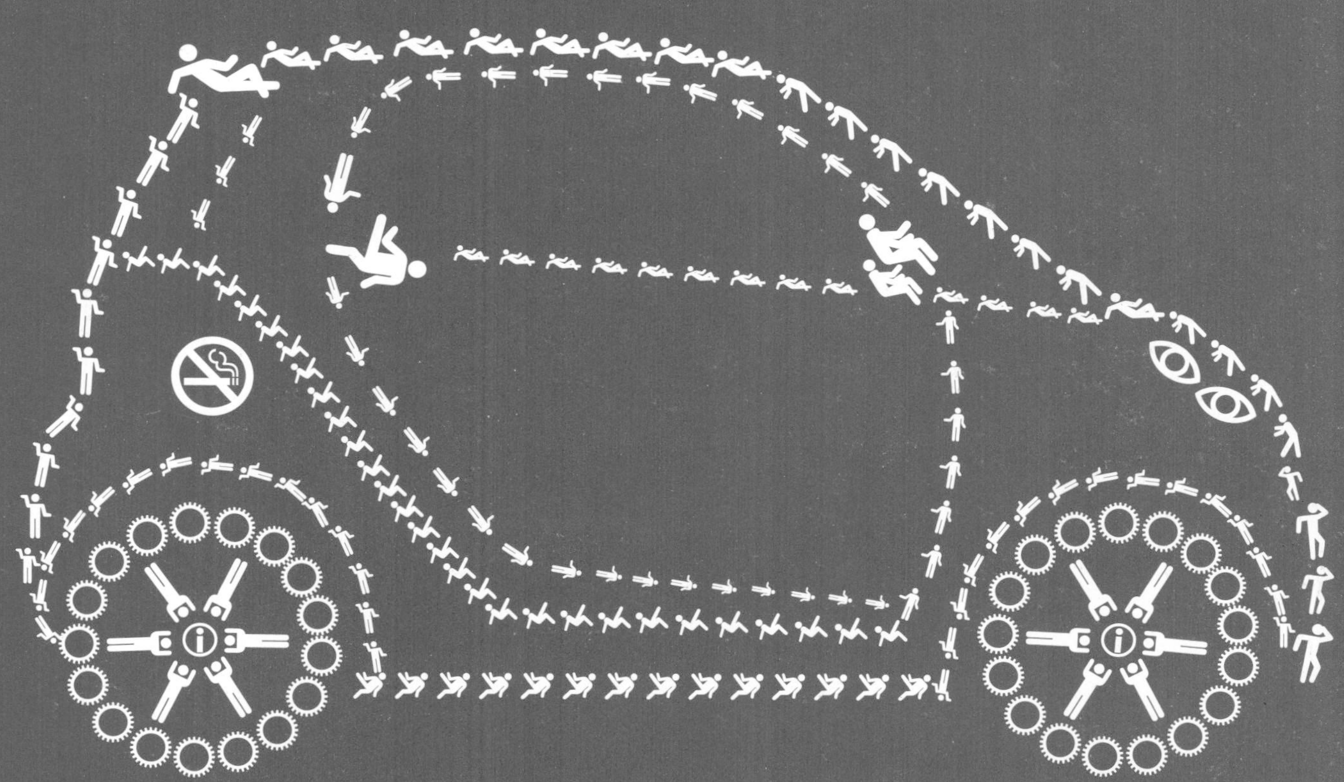

smart fortwo, New York, Times Square

smart

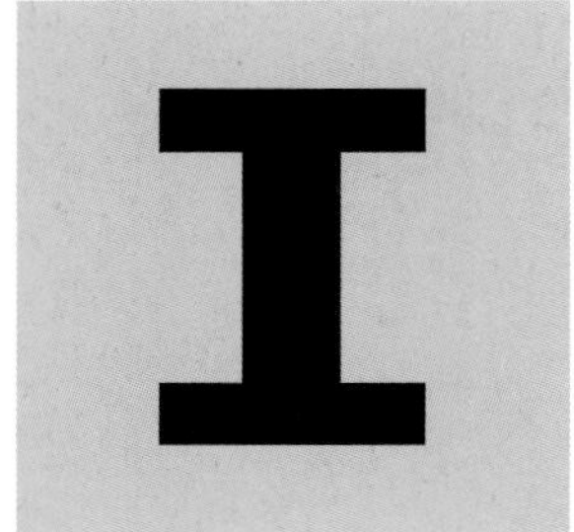

HISTORY & TECHNOLOGY

CITY
CITY

BROADWAY
W 45 ST
ONE WAY
ONE WAY
CLEARCHANNEL
SPECTACOLOR
Marriott
MARQUIS
FlashDancers
4G34
7G33
5M27
All Beef Hot Dogs
WAIT FOR WALK

Kodak
maxell
ONE WAY
"High-voltage Virtuosity!"
NO STOPPING ANYTIME
NEW YORK Marriott MARQUIS
MARQUIS
MARQUIS THEATRE BOX OFFICE
WINNER! BEST MUSICAL
OFF DUTY 7E82 OFF DUTY
W 45 St
GEORGE
4L38A

1:43.41
30 CPL 92

smart
D-MCFK

Mammut

DAIMLERCHRYSLER
a smart new addition to
the Detroit Fire Department

TRIKETEC

FOLLOW ME
B 045004

forfun

POLIZIA

1:31.56
861 BWL 78

forfun²
smart

39

FOLLOW ME
BB F 1399

metallbau
KI FIRE 5

M SK 6666

FK 9

www.smart-camper.com
TS HX 118

sm

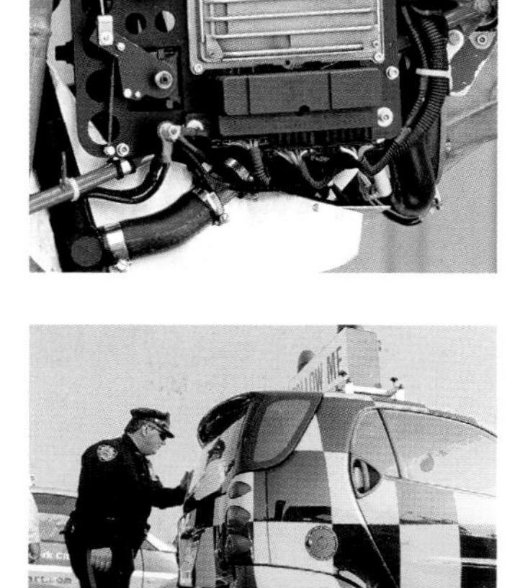

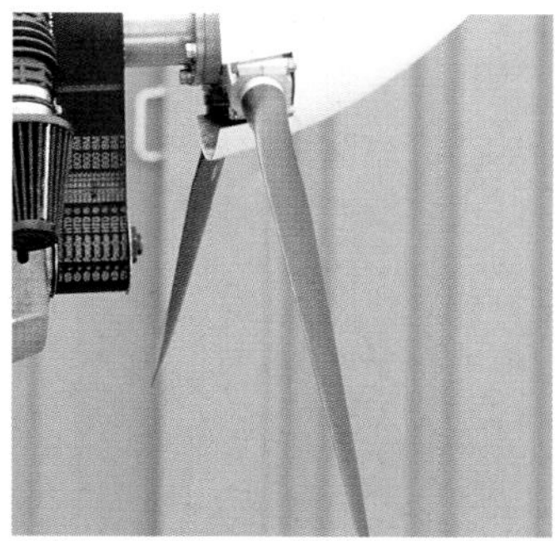

BL CD 11

Jürgen Zöllter

I.I THE SMART STORY: "REDUCE TO THE MAX"

- 1997: The city car of the future becomes reality
- The smart fortwo is the logical answer to many questions of mobility
- Practical means of transportation, cult object, and urban icon, all in one
- First concepts for a highly compact, economical two-seater

Stuttgart. Extremely compact, highly innovative, and self-consciously individualistic: the smart city coupe made a radical break with 20th century automotive convention. The vehicle – today, known as the smart fortwo – was first shown to the public at the 1997 Frankfurt International Automobile Show. Simultaneously, the show marked the debut of the smart marque, as part of Daimler-Benz.

The two-seater provided very unique answers to questions of individual mobility, above all in urban centers. For example, it took up very little space, and exhibited low fuel consumption combined with minimal carbon dioxide emissions, yet it could transport two occupants and their luggage to their destination in high comfort and in the greatest possible safety.

In 1997, even as most mobility issues seemed to lie in a far-distant future, consistent implementation of the smart already presented an obvious solution. To date, there had never been a car anywhere in the world so thoroughly thought out, and taking up so little space. Since 1998, customers in 36 countries have chosen this unique vehicle; in all, 770,256 examples of the first-generation smart fortwo were built between 1997 and 2006.

Since then, many future challenges have manifested themselves in the here and now. The second generation of the smart fortwo entered the marketplace in April 2007, offering even better solutions. No other enterprise can point to such comprehensive experience in this vehicle class as DaimlerChrysler. As an integral part of the industry, the firm has been writing automotive history for more than 120 years, since its founding in 1886; in that time, it has filled that history with innovative design solutions for personal mobility. The history of smart is short, but colorful. In 1998, the gasoline-powered smart city coupe entered the market, followed in 1999 by its diesel variant. Later, the smart cabrio rounded out the model line, followed by the smart roadster, smart roadster coupe and smart forfour – which, today, are all history, for the market has concentrated on the original configuration of the car, as the perfect solution to many pressing problems of personal mobility.

The smart fortwo is an established cult car in many of the world's metropolitan areas. The weekly newspaper Die Zeit calls this vehicle concept an *"urban icon,"* setting benchmarks for innovative mobility, consistent application of new technology, and a design that lends visual emphasis to constructive details. The second generation of the smart fortwo carries on in the tradition of its predecessor, as the fascinating history of smart continues.

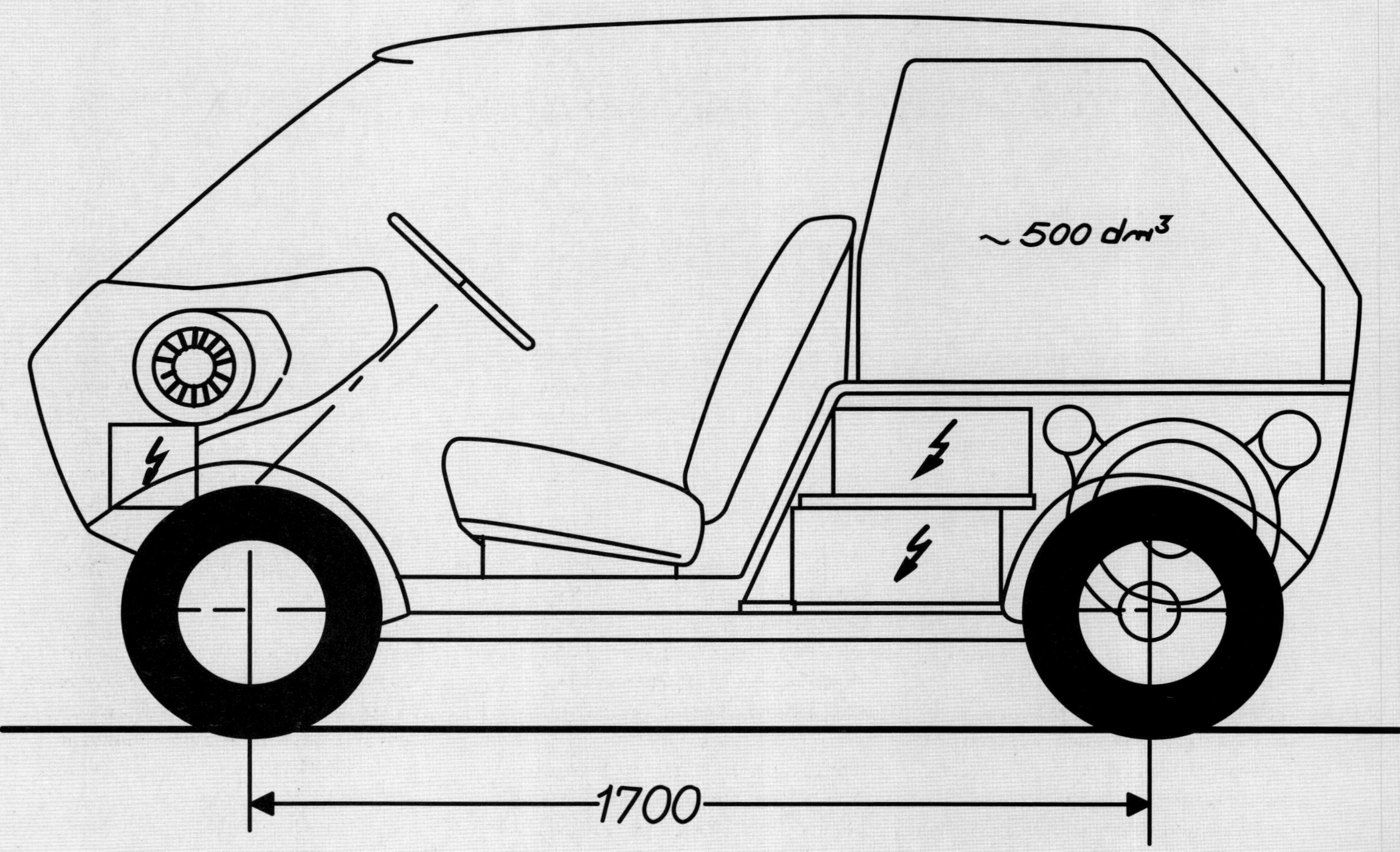

Tomforde
Concept sketch, 1972

Jürgen Zöllter

I.2 BEGINNINGS: A LOOK BACK TO THE YEAR 1972

- In 1972, Mercedes creates its first compact car study for the year 2000
- From the NAFA urban commuter concept to the Mercedes City Car
- An overall vehicle length of 2.5 meters is a prerequisite

The beginnings of smart development reach back 35 years. In the early 1970s, Mercedes-Benz began work on a design study for the automotive future of the year 2000. Research and farsighted development have always played an important role at Mercedes-Benz. These activities demand creative people with well-grounded knowledge of future traffic development, a sense for trends, and a good measure of fantasy. The countless Mercedes-Benz innovations which have gone from design studies and experimental vehicles into volume production represent an expression of the successful work of such futurists.

Traditionally, the advanced thinkers of Mercedes-Benz live at least ten years ahead of the times. However, the compact car project was oriented nearly three decades into the future.

This extraordinary, visionary planning was spurred by the 1973 oil crisis, which, in Europe, even resulted in driving bans. From such experiences, and estimation of future traffic growth, engineers at Mercedes-Benz formulated a requirement for an especially fuel-efficient and compact vehicle for the cities of the future. Responsibility for the project was vested in Johann Tomforde, at the time Mercedes-Benz project leader responsible for future transportation systems.

On October 6, 1972, Tomforde wrote Werner Breitschwerdt, at the time deputy director at Mercedes-Benz and responsible for experimental passenger car bodies. In his letter, engineer Tomforde predicted a fundamental change in individual mobility in urban areas. The automobile, in its present form, would no longer make sense for all traffic areas; Tomforde estimated „the relationship of the present automobile to future traffic systems... [would depend on] the possible function of the automobile as part of a newly conceived, optimized traffic system." The development potential of the cars of 1972 was correspondingly high.

Development of future Mercedes-Benz passenger cars would have to be concentrated on ride and driving comfort, progressive safety, and environmental responsibility.

MCC concept
Parking area reduction: 50%
Parking lane reduction: 70%

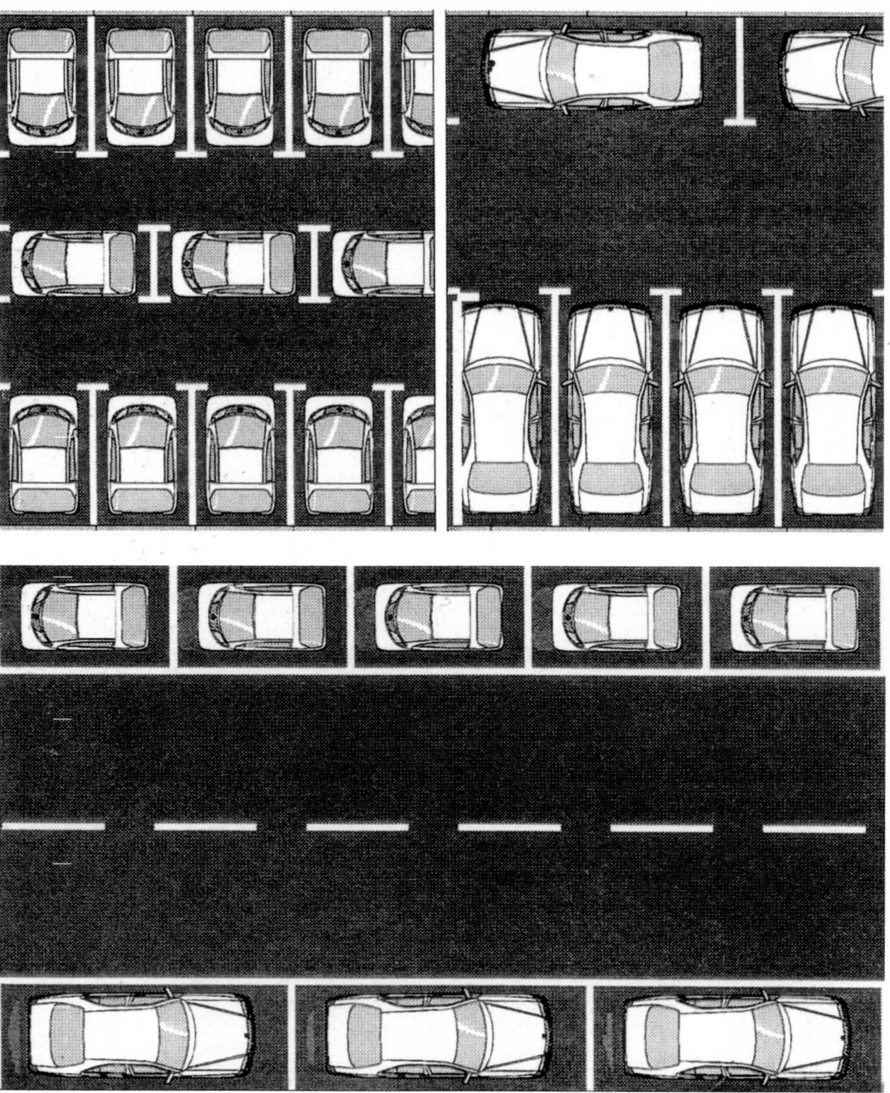

MCC concept
Truck loading
Rail loading

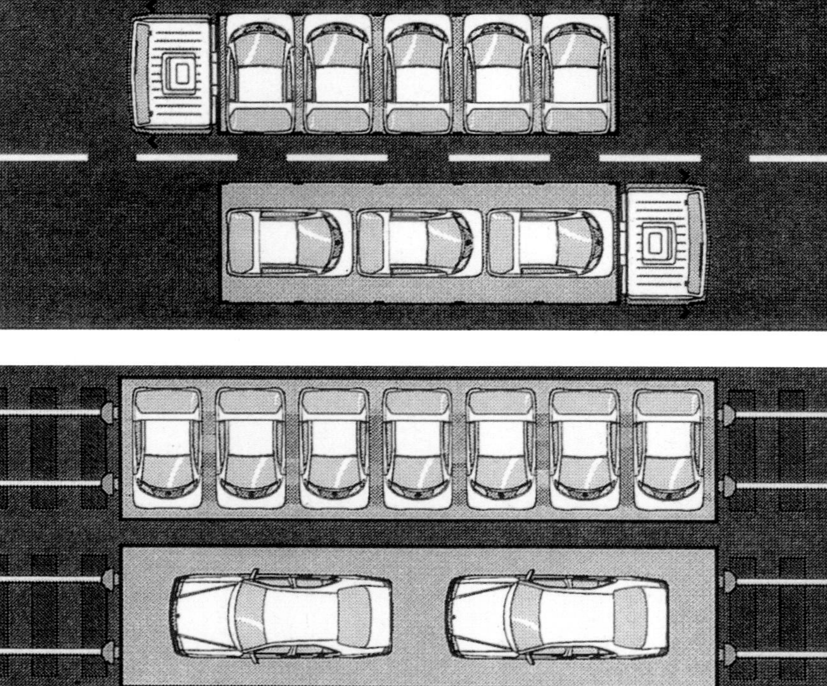

MCC concept
Lane width utilization (compact car lane)

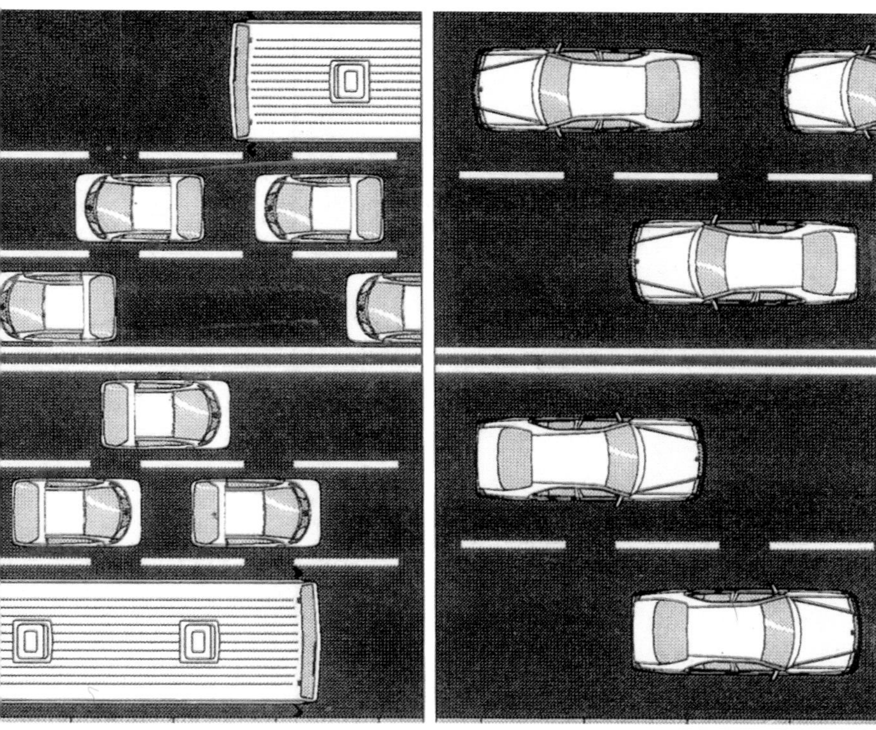

MCC concept
Lane width reduction: 70%

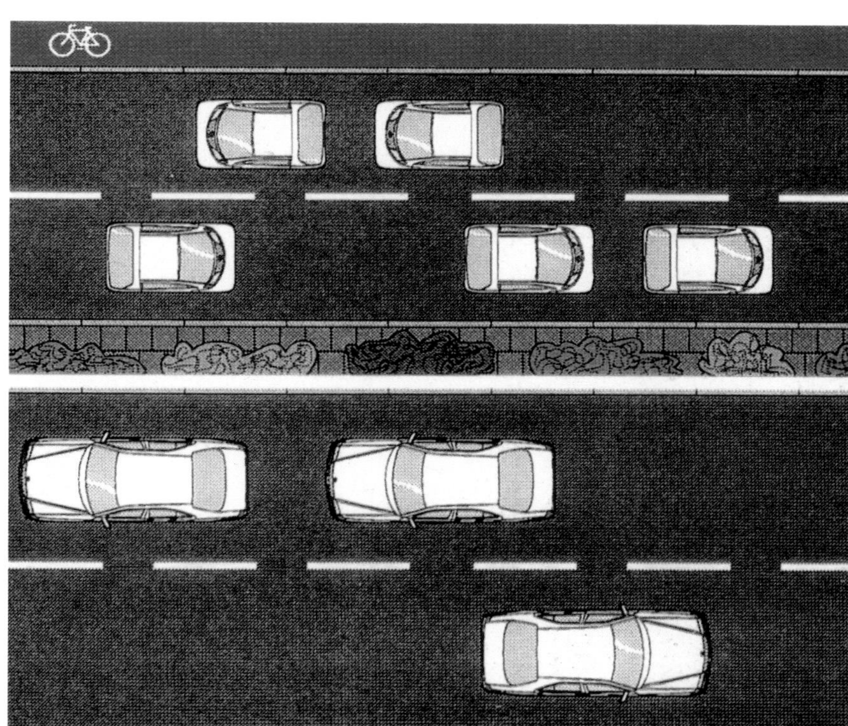

The project team had already developed a vision for ensuring mobility in urban areas: a 2.5 meter long two-seater with luggage compartment, on a wheelbase of only 1.70 meters. This basic outline already sounded like the future smart. Accordingly, the drawings showed a short-nosed, "one box" design. This compact car was not intended to carry a combustion engine under its hood, but rather electric drive, with energy storage at the rear of the vehicle. Other drivetrain variations were subsequently developed, including the so-called „Dual Car" with hybrid drive.

On the basis of the design sketches, the team developed a driveable, tube frame seating buck. This rough model was intended to convince skeptics that superior economy of space could be achieved even in a microcompact vehicle. After all, if such a small car were to be sent forth to revolutionize the automotive world, it would have to have not only great manageability, but also offer the comfort of a modern Mercedes-Benz; in the words of Tomforde, "as expected by our present customer base."

Initially, the visionary small car concept faltered. The blame may be placed not on its economy of space, but rather on vehicle safety; in 1972, it was not yet clear which engineering measures would be needed to meet the in-house standards of Mercedes-Benz' safety research department with such a compact vehicle.

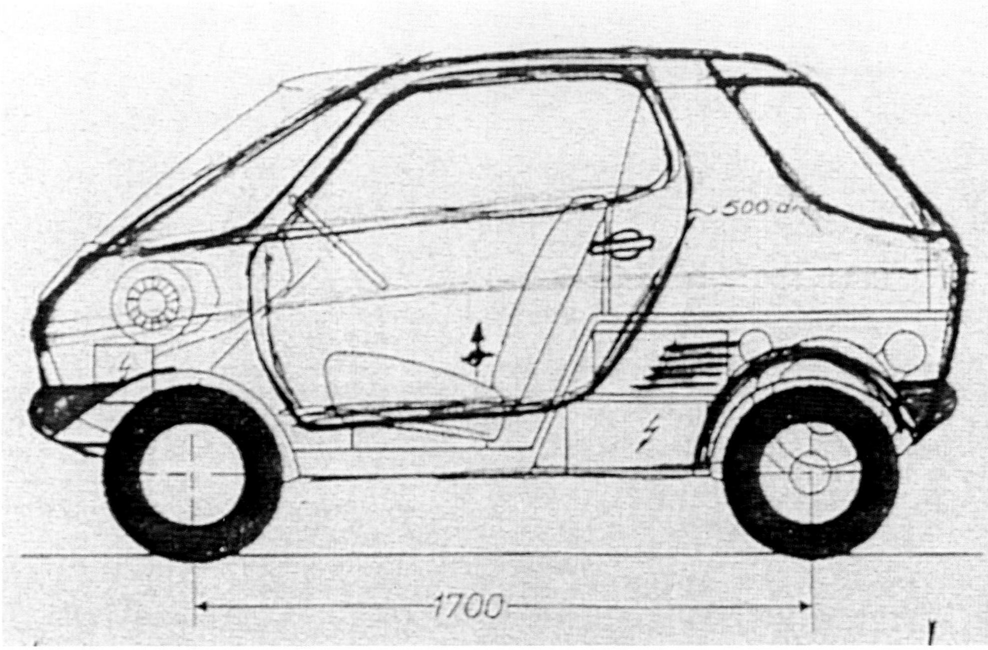

[1]

A look back at the history of the time shows how revolutionary the new concept must have appeared. In 1972, a Mercedes-Benz was either an S-class automobile or a midrange model. Customers who enjoyed successful careers and cultivated a stylish, active lifestyle might choose a Mercedes-Benz SL sports car. Heads of state and captains of industry, on the other hand, were chauffeured in the Type 600, the Stuttgart automaker's prestigious limousine. Each of these vehicles, in its own way, incorporated the elegance, high level of flair and operating comfort, occupant protection and durability that was expected of a Mercedes-Benz.

These vehicles reflected those qualities which make up the marque's acknowledged high level of competence. At that time, it would have been difficult to imagine that more compact market segments would someday also be represented within the circle of vehicles proudly wearing the three-pointed star. Imagining a compact car, only two and a half meters long, with new body shapes and a futuristic drive system, would have represented nothing less than a revolution.

[1] First sketch, 1972

1981: NAHVERKEHRSFAHRZEUG (NAFA) – THE "LOCAL TRAFFIC VEHICLE"

[2]

Despite these objections, Mercedes-Benz engineers continued to pursue this visionary concept. Nine years later, they presented a concept study, the NAFA "Nahverkehrsfahrzeug" ("Local Traffic Vehicle"). Developed in 1981, the car represented a more focused interpretation of the basic idea of 1972, providing an answer to overcrowded roads, lack of parking space, and traffic jams.

The advanced development team, which included young college graduate Gerhard Steinle as a newly-minted Mercedes designer, was presented with a six-page list of project requirements which the study would need to satisfy. These included the ability to park at right angles to traffic flow without presenting an obstacle to moving traffic.

After numerous design studies on paper and in clay, a driveable full-size prototype was built and presented to the public: 2.5 meters long, 1.5 meters wide and tall. Weighing only 550 kg (1210 lbs.), the compact vehicle was propelled by a 41 horsepower (30 kW) three-cylinder, one-liter engine, driving through the front wheels and an automatic transmission. Intelligent solutions for perfect urban ergonomics included sliding doors, which permitted comfortable entry and egress. Thanks to all-wheel steering, with electrically actuated rear wheel steering allowing up to 15 degrees of lock, the car's turning circle was only 5.7 meters, and it could be parallel parked without backing, by pulling forward into tight parking spaces.

[3]

[4]

Its comprehensive equipment list included air conditioning, power steering and seat belt tensioners.

This product of advanced engineering development was grounds for optimism: the NAFA car met the conditions for a low-emissions city car with a small traffic footprint, yet offered outstanding economy of space. Would Mercedes-Benz produce such a car in the foreseeable future? Alas, as in 1972, the decision

[2] Vehicle dynamics test mule, 1981/82
[3] Sketch, 1981/82
[4] NAFA entry model, 1981/82

[1]

[2]

against going into production was based on the marque's stringent safety requirements for its own vehicles, even though the NAFA sported controlled-deformation body components as well as rigid side impact protection and an automatic belt system. Undoubtedly, another contributing factor was a contemporary market survey, which indicated that there was limited enthusiasm for such a compact car. Surveys concluded that consumer desires tended more toward large, powerful automobiles.

Despite the second oil crisis, this anticipated trend did indeed materialize, and did not diminish until the late 1980s. When the California state government announced its intention to apply the Clean Air Act to combat Los Angeles' chronic smog problem, it set in motion a global dynamic. Worldwide, public awareness of air pollution as a problem increased in urban areas, and led to additional regulations. In Italy, governments successively closed off historic city centers to internal combustion vehicles; Singapore dramatically increased its vehicle license fees; and Tokyo allowed inner-city car registrations only if owners could prove they had a parking space.

During this phase of public debate, Mercedes-Benz seized the initiative, for an easily imposed prohibition against individual traffic in urban areas did not represent an acceptable perspective for ensuring, on the one hand, people's mobility and supply interests, and on the other, for improving air quality in cities. Mercedes-Benz therefore oriented its innovative individual inner-city mobility concept to the time frame of the California Clean Air Act.

At the time, California required that by 2002, each significant automotive marque doing business in the California market offer at least ten percent of its model line as "Zero Emissions Vehicles," so-called ZEVs.

1990: Work begins on the Mercedes city car

As a first step, in 1988, Mercedes-Benz advanced development engineers converted the two-seater NAFA to electric propulsion and a high-energy battery. The researchers considered a pilot project with up to 100 electric NAFA cars for West Berlin, but battery capacity was as yet inadequate for such continuous duty. On this basis, two mutually cooperating project teams were established in early 1990, to derive two different concepts from the NAFA study and to develop these to the point of production readiness. One team developed the five-seat Vision A 93 prototype, first shown to the public at the 1993 IAA (Frankfurt International Auto Show). In 1994, with slight modifications, this car was shown as "Study A," and represented the direct ancestor of the Mercedes-Benz A-Class. The other group worked on the concept of the "Mercedes City Car" respectively Micro Compact Car (MCC), a two-seater with cargo space. Special features of the project included electric front-wheel drive and high-performance energy storage in an intermediate space below the seats.

These concepts turned out rather tall, resulting in a comparatively high seating position for the occupants, which in turn required a high roofline.

With the MCC, the responsible project team accepted one of the greatest challenges ever presented to Mercedes-Benz vehicle development: to achieve, in a micro-compact electric car only 2.5 meters long, all the virtues and qualities of a genuine Mercedes, including occupant protection and depth of innovation. Full-scale design drawings were presented to designer Anton Reichel and his "Team 1990" in Sindelfingen.

Reichel's responsibility was mentoring and supervision of the project's engineering development. But what about exterior and interior design? The solution was simultaneously radical and harmonious.

[1] Johann Tomforde with quarter-scale MCC model, 1992
[2] MCC sketch, 1992
[3] Mercedes design chief Bruno Sacco with MCC eco sprinter and NAFA

[3]

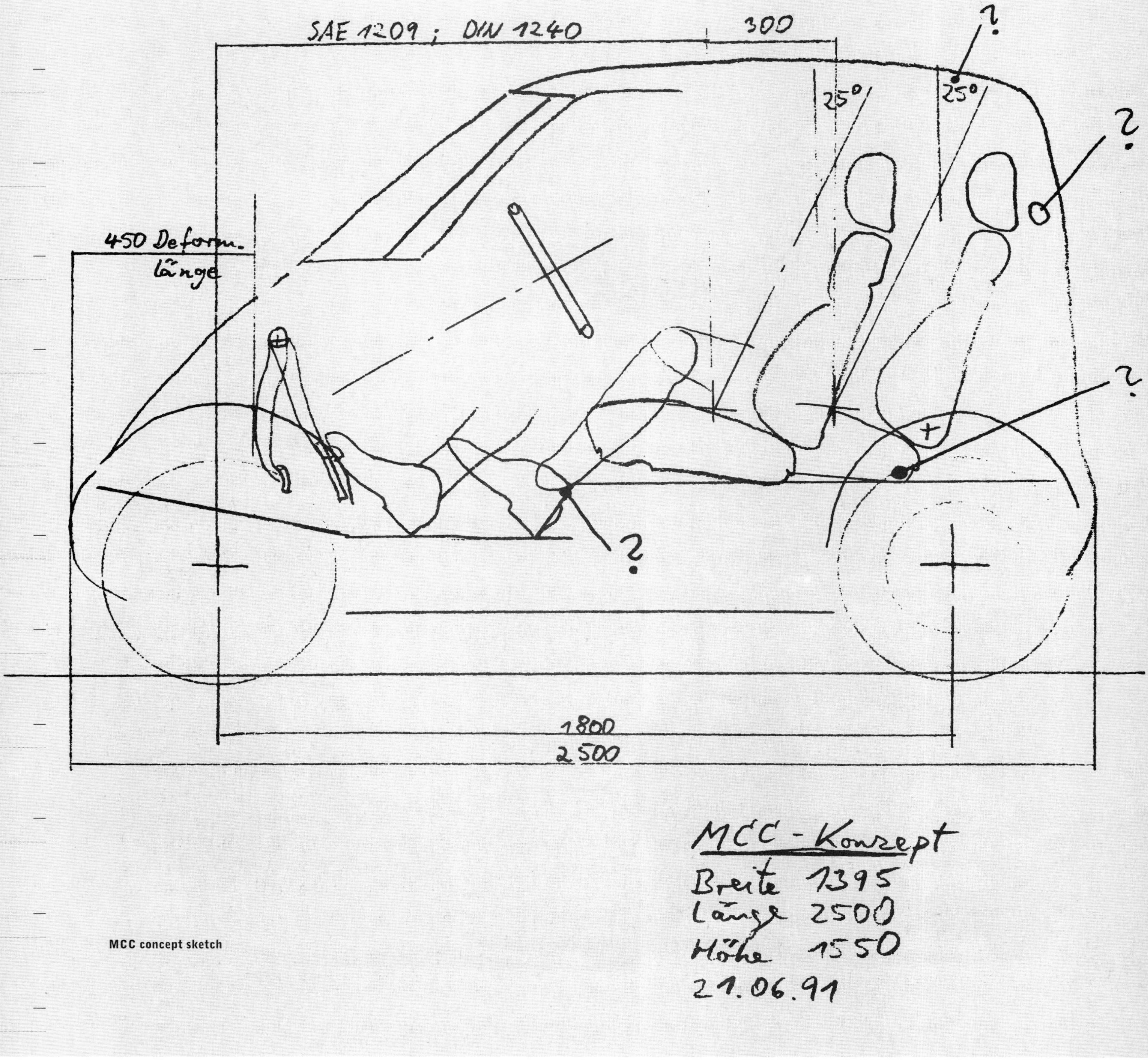

SAE 1209 ; DIN 1240

300

25°

25°

450 Deform.
länge

1800

2500

MCC - Konzept

Breite 1395

Länge 2500

Höhe 1550

21.06.91

MCC concept sketch

Jürgen Zöllter

1.3 IDEA MINING IN NORTH AMERICA

- 1991: Design development of the MCC 01 begins in California
- First prototypes provide an exciting prospect
- An ecological vehicle concept enters the program

The new compact car would be designed in the United States. In early 1990, Mercedes-Benz designer Gerhard Steinle, representing design chief Bruno Sacco, flew to the States to scout suitable locations for the planned Mercedes-Benz Advanced Design exterior studio. Steinle decided on Irvine, in southern California, some of the world's most fertile ground for automobile trend research. Here, auto aficionados, with their historic as well as modern, but almost always highly individualistic cars, could experience a true cult of mobility on wheels.

In 1991, Mercedes chief designer Bruno Sacco issued the first assignment to the newly recruited design team, all graduates of the renown Art Center College of Design in Pasadena. Their mission was to grapple with the two-seat microcompact car, now internally designated the MCC 01. Actually, the young designers had hoped to be allowed to create exciting roadsters and elegant sport coupes for Mercedes-Benz. But they had been chosen deliberately for this project by the responsible staff in Stuttgart.

After all, the design of the Mercedes City Car was to be the product of people who experienced the problems of urban mobility firsthand – for example, as in many cities of southern California.

The design team around Gerhard Steinle always strove to find a connection to the reality of everyday urban mobility. To this end, the team developed its solutions not only in their offices and studios, but also went on frequent field trips to the liveliest parts of the surrounding towns. On a weekly basis, designers took excursions to the sidewalk cafés of Newport Beach and Laguna Beach, to Sunset Boulevard in nearby Los Angeles, and to Huntington

Left: The Mercedes-Benz board of directors visiting the California design studio, 1994.

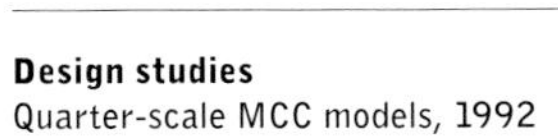

Design studies
Quarter-scale MCC models, 1992

Beach. They spent afternoons in Malibu and Santa Monica, over milkshakes and drafting paper, with Italian espresso and a brace of pencils.

The designers got close to the public, observed their interactions with the automobile in everyday service: who used which vehicles for what purpose? What tasks do drivers have to struggle with, what is important to them in which situations – entering the car, opening a convertible top, loading the trunk, installing child seats, eating and drinking in the car, applying makeup and shaving?

From the resulting flood of impressions, the design team distilled its first renderings. Gerhard Steinle recalls that at first, there was a concept for a rather pudgy city car. To observers, the models appeared as long as they were wide and tall; these proportions simply didn't "look right." Therefore, an important task from the outset was to reinforce a visual impression of vehicle length.

Among other things, this was achieved by reducing width from 1.68 meters to 1.40 meters, which moved the seats closer together. To offer occupants the same freedom of motion as found in the front seats of the Mercedes-Benz C-class, the designers of Irvine recalled the F 100 research vehicle, with its staggered front seat arrangement. After conferring with their colleagues in Sindelfingen, a similar configuration was developed for the MCC 01.

1992: Prototypes are built

On July 4, 1992, the Mercedes management board accepted the full-scale model, with its staggered seating arrangement. Jürgen Hubbert signed the contract for a driveable prototype, which would be built for the teams in Irvine and Sindelfingen by Metalcrafters, an independent automotive prototype shop near the Mercedes-Benz Advanced Design Studios. Many detail considerations were developed immediately afterwards, at a barbecue under starlit southern California skies.

Bruno Sacco's decision to create the Mercedes City Car in southern California, far from the home office, provided its developers a certain degree of independence, compared to the studios in Stuttgart. In addition, stylistic and aesthetic trends from the Los Angeles megalopolis, with its ever-changing society, flowed into the work. Mercedes designer Paul Terry took advantage of this freedom to draw a second MCC, a convertible, based on the existing concept.

This MCC Cabriolet excited his colleagues; the design team worked out renderings of the model, and presented the design in Sindelfingen, while in Irvine, the clay model of the MCC 01 was transformed into a convertible. Bruno Sacco gave the green light for a convertible as a second prototype. Again, building the actual vehicle was entrusted to Metalcrafters.

[1]

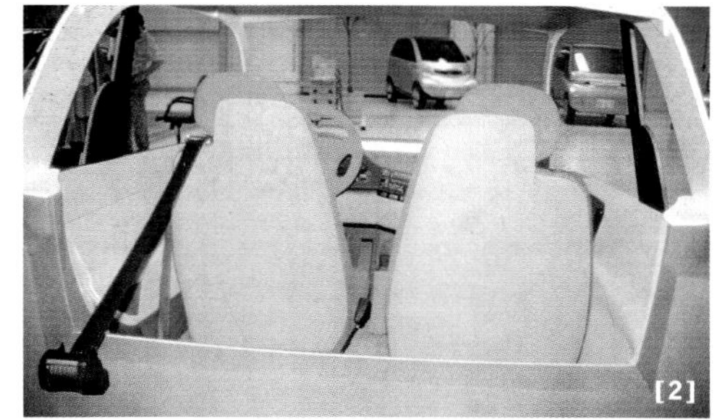
[2]

[3]

[4]

1993: Eco Sprinter and Eco Speedster

In 1993, two show cars, based on the prototypes, were created. The coupe was transformed into the "Eco Sprinter," a more serious, black-painted variation with leather and wood interior trim. The Cabrio, on the other hand, metamorphosed into the "Eco Speedster," a youthful, dynamic version of the Mercedes City Car. The Speedster made a striking visual impact, with its bright yellow paintwork and an almost pop-art inspired interior, with blue, red, green and yellow elements. The vehicle was clearly aimed at a young, creative audience. The shape of both reworked prototypes, presented to the Mercedes-Benz board of directors, already hinted at the future smart fortwo.

The two MCC prototypes owed their broad acceptance as completely novel city vehicles, and as part of an innovative mobility concept, to the wealth of ideas offered by Mercedes-Benz designers in Irvine and Sindelfingen. Their creativity grew in the course of a steady exchange between continents, and also led to a lively trade in workplace locations; the Stuttgart crew valued the working atmosphere in California. Bernhard Joseph, at the time responsible for cockpit ergonomics, recalls that team conferences were often held under the southern California sun.

Individual and team decisions were made not only in the office, but also in "Re Nato," a beachfront restaurant in Newport Beach; on the way to "C'est Si Bon," a local French bakery; or on mountain bike excursions to Top of the World Drive, an outdoor activity destination on a hill overlooking Laguna Beach. Such locations provided designers with their inspiration.

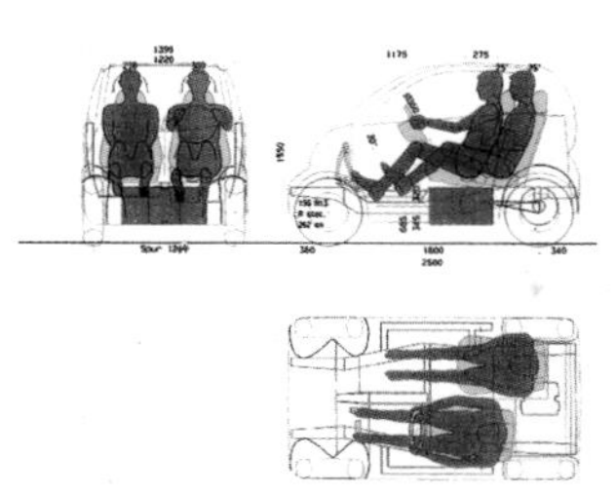

[5]

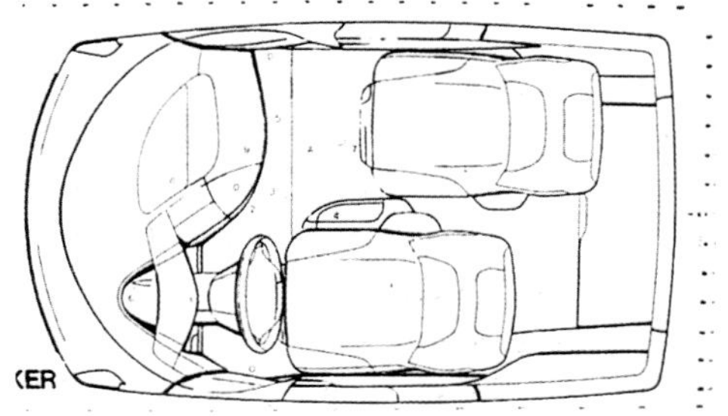
[6]

[1–4] MCC 01, clay and interior models, 1992
[5] MCC package drawing, 1992
[6] Interior plan view tape drawing, 1992

MCC eco-sprinter, 1993

MCC eco-speedster, 1993

speedster

VOL
MODE
TUNE

smart entry mockup, 1995
Left: interior design variations

Interior study, Frankfurt Auto Show, 1995

Jürgen Zöllter

I.4 COOPERATION: SWATCH AND MERCEDES-BENZ JOIN FORCES

- 1992: First encounter with Nicolas G. Hayek
- Micro Compact Car AG is founded
- A manufacturing plant is built in France

While the Micro Car was being developed in the United States, Mercedes-Benz AG board chairman Werner Niefer received a visitor. This encounter between Niefer and management consultant Nicolas G. Hayek, on December 3, 1992, would have a decisive effect on development of the MCC. After phenomenal marketplace success with his "Swatch" wristwatch, Hayek, a Lebanese-American mathematician and physicist, wanted to build a visionary city car.

Hayek, who had almost single-handedly rejuvenated the Swiss watch industry, did not dare to undertake such a venture alone. But he was confident that with the right partner from the auto industry, the project would succeed. His ability to discern trends is witnessed by his Société de Microélectronique et d'Horlogerie (Swiss Society for Microelectronics and Watchmaking AG, SMH). This concern, today known as the Swatch Group with headquarters in Biel, has since 1984 been the driving force behind resurgence of the Swiss watch industry to once again lead the world market.

In early 1993, Hayek believed that the manufacturing strategies he had developed for the watch industry in the early 1980s could be applied to automobile manufacturing.

Hayek dreamed of a city car for personal transportation in urban areas, a car whose environmental responsibility and functionality would be as compelling as its quality and value-for-money. Furthermore, the car was to be integrated in networked systems to ensure geographically extensive and politically opportune individual mobility.

Volkswagen's chairman of the board, Ferdinand Piëch, examined Hayek's considerations, but decided to go his own way toward the small car of the future. In 1991, Piëch's predecessors, Carl Hahn and VW brand chief Daniel Goeudevert had decided on a 50 percent stake for VW in a SMH Volkswagen AG, with the object of building a Swatch automobile. Piëch, however, bailed out of the project upon taking over the chairmanship in Wolfsburg.

Werner Niefer, on the other hand, showed great interest in Hayek's vision, and invited the head of Mercedes-Benz' passenger car division, Jürgen Hubbert, to take part in the meeting. Just five months earlier, Hubbert had issued the contract for building the prototype of the two-seater developed by Mercedes-Benz. As they parted company, the

[1]

Mercedes managers assured Hayek that they give the topic serious consideration.

The time was ripe for Hayek's idea, for in the late 1980s, the European auto industry was undergoing a sea change in its production methods. New strategies were needed to increase value creation in the face of rising complexity and market dynamics. Car manufacturers were searching for a silver bullet to make automobile production both more flexible and more economical. This, among other things, led to strategic alliances between carmakers and the supplier industries. At the end, it was realized that manufacturing steps that resulted in variations would have to be incorporated in larger units, so-called modules; the auto industry moved toward a platform strategy. Mercedes-Benz, too, was affected by this transformation. Moreover, at the time,

[2]

Daimler-Benz AG was in the process of reorientation, as CEO Edzard Reuter was pushing the tradition-laden Stuttgart firm to shift from being purely an automobile manufacturer into developing as an integrated technology company.

1993: Electric drive for the Micro Compact Car?

On January 3, 1993, at their second meeting in Stuttgart, Nicolas Hayek presented his development plans, which documented research work on electric vehicle drives carried out at Switzerland's Biel School of Engineering. From the outset, it was Hayek's objective to build an electric car. In parallel, research projects at the watchmaker's Biel headquarters got underway to explore new avenues in networking automotive electrics and electronics.

Werner Niefer resolved to travel to Biel with a small delegation, in order to observe the activities firsthand. In early February 1993, the delegation visited a workshop in SMH's headquarters building in Biel, staffed by a team of technicians as well as a prototype body.

Jürgen Hubbert refers to what they found as "a small, patched-together contraption with all manner of electronic components and four electric hub motors." Nicolas Hayek presented the 2.5 meter long electric car to his visitors; loaded with engineering refinements, it was equipped to do battle with small-car competitors from Japan. Like the example set by his modular Swatch watches, Hayek intended

[3]

to use standardized, miniaturized assemblies, for example the electronic control systems for powertrain and suspension jointly developed by SMH and the Biel School of Engineering.

Hayek suggested that the additional costs incurred for these modular assemblies would be made up by savings in the body structure. Back in Stuttgart and Sindelfingen, intensive discussions took place within Mercedes' development departments, the bone of contention being occupant protection, which, for a small car, would demand complex body structures – diametrically opposite Hayek's desires to save costs in this department. The engineers contended that compact wheel hub motors for Hayek's electric all-wheel drive were technically feasible, but by no means within the cost framework of an affordable automobile.

Regardless of dissenting voices, Niefer and Hayek announced their next summit meeting: again, with only a small, select group, during the March, 1993 Geneva Auto Salon, where Niefer decided: "We'll do it!"

1994: The founding of Micro Compact Car AG

Looking back, it appears that Niefer, who would soon retire from his post as Mercedes-Benz chairman, was establishing a legacy, to be institutionalized in stages by his successor, Helmut Werner, beginning in May 1993.

The two show cars were presented to the press in March, 1994: the Eco Sprinter coupe, powered by a 40 kW electric motor, and the Eco Speedster convertible, with a three-cylinder gasoline engine like that which would eventually power the smart. Both show cars were rear-wheel drive, with an engine/transmission unit installed in an underfloor configuration. This, too, would enter production with the smart. In April, Micro Compact Car AG (MCC) was established as a joint venture between Daimler-Benz AG of Stuttgart and the Schweizerische Gesellschaft für Mikroelektronik und Uhrenindustrie (Swiss Corporation for Microelectronics and Watchmaking Industries Ltd), SMH,

[1] Optimizing the exterior in the wind tunnel
[2] In the car, Werner (left) and Hayek (right), Sarreguemines, France, 1995.
[3] Early sketches of the smart fortwo

[1]

in Biel. Daimler-Benz controlled a 51 percent share of MCC, while SMH held the remaining 49 percent. The long-term goal of the joint venture was to transform the vision of a new generation of mobility systems into reality. Hayek dreamed of a fleet of economically produced, brightly colored miniature automobiles, as colorful as his wristwatches. But the Stuttgart engineers warned the watchmaker: the development yardstick would be the carmaker's safety requirements. A cheap car could not be realized on this level, and therefore was not desirable. Therefore, the first product to be developed to production-ready status would not be Hayek's planned Swatchmobile, but rather the smart microcar, based on the Eco Sprinter.

On the one hand, the name of the new model represented a cute, intelligent car for the 21st century, but also spoke of the concept's origins: **S**watch **M**ercedes **Art**. This decision punctuated the two partners' conflicting goals, which also included the propulsion system. Hayek, supported by research at the Hochschule für Technik und Information (College of Technology and Information), HTI, in

Biel, favored the electric city car; his Swatch cars were to obtain their power through electric motors and hybrid drives.

In contrast, Mercedes-Benz' engineers believed in the potential of gasoline and diesel propulsion. A decision would be determined by experiment: in mid-1994, to demonstrate the advantages of wheel hub motors, the Swiss staged a driving demonstration on Biel's ice stadium. A driving course was marked out on the ice track, allowing drivers to experience the maneuverability and traction advantages of all-wheel drive (which could be easily realized with wheel hub motors). But the demonstration was a failure, and the decision of Mercedes-Benz representatives was unanimous: this vehicle was not roadworthy.

[1] interior concept car, Atlanta, 1996
[2] modular concept car, Paris, 1996

1994: The decision to build the smart

With that, the last hurdle standing in the path of the smart's development was removed. Years of research work on Mercedes-Benz' own small car projects fell into place in the new vehicle concept. The project was once again shepherded by Johann Tomforde, the same engineer who had thought of just such a concept as far back as 1972. The smart would be an entirely new vehicle concept for urban centers; a subcompact two-seater, targeted at a completely new market segment for the auto industry: the smart class.

Ultimately, the two-seater was brought to production readiness by MCC GmbH in Renningen, near Stuttgart, a wholly-owned subsidiary of MCC AG of Biel. Johann Tomforde served as director of development and production; Jörg Schär, who had come from Swatch, was in charge of marketing and building a distribution organization; and Christoph Baubin handled finances. Jürgen Hubbert served as president of the MCC AG board of directors, with Nicolas Hayek as vice president. Management meetings took place on a regular basis beginning in mid-1994, attended by Helmut Werner, Jürgen Hubbert and Dieter Zetsche of Mercedes. Sitting opposite were Nicolas Hayek and his partners. Even as Hayek, the initiator of the project, came to have ever less influence on development of the vehicle, he became more involved as creative director in planning the smart's completely novel production methods. His experiences in dealing with modular manufacturing technology resulted in controversial discussions, but, ultimately, for "smart" solutions.

A committed design team, under the direction of former Mercedes-Benz designer Jens Manske, needed just under three years from concept to realization. Beginning with a small office, the team quickly grew to the MCC design department. Modelmaker Martin Karl directed construction of the first quarter-scale clay models. A full-size model was completed in time for the design presentation in September 1994.

The smart is to be built in France

In December 1994, the Daimler-Benz AG board of directors decided that the new car would be built in Hambach-Sarreguemines, in the French province of Lorraine. To this end, a new entity was created, MCC France SAS, to undertake production of the smart in a completely new industrial park in Hambach, beginning in 1997.

The French subsidiary began with a capitalization of 100 million French francs. Daimler-Benz participation was 38.3 percent, while the SMH Group held 36.7 percent. SOFIREM (Société Financière pour favoriser l'Industrialisation des Régions Minières) held the remaining 25 percent, with 25 million francs, as an investment, not a subsidy. As a government body, SOFIREM's mission was to promote this structurally threatened coal mining area of France, and it entered the scene as a venture partner of MCC France. SOFIREM made significant contributions to integration of MCC France into the industrial landscape of the Lorraine region, and helped establish valuable business contacts on the regional as well as national level.

[1] Press conference in the Mercedes Museum, 1994: l to r, Zetsche, Hubbert, Werner, Hayek
[2] Press conference in Sarreguemines, 1995: in the car, l to r, Tomforde, Baubin, Schär
[3] A motorcycle frame as inspiration for the tridion idea

1995: model approval for the smart

The design model was approved by the MCC management board in April 1995. For Jens Manske's design team, this represented the most significant step toward series production, and the scene was set accordingly: roller skaters circled a hastily built stage, acrobats performed, and boom boxes pounded out music. The spectacle set the tone for the invited guests, carried them off into the youthful milieu of the customers in whose hands the MCC designers envisioned their new automobile. For them, the smart is no mere thought experiment, but rather a car with body and soul: trendy, but also polarizing, a being with character. And near the end of the show, when Jens Manske started the tiny electric motor and turned a few laps with the hard model, the result was spontaneous enthusiasm. In the guests' applause, the designers heard absolute approval: their proposal had been accepted, their toil had been rewarded, the smart was on its way.

The MCC design department had raised the smart to be a character car. Its personality came alive in the many details which its youthful designers had brought in from their personal lifestyles. Whether it was their fondness for motorcycles, empathy for powerful or impertinent comic book heroes, the viewing habits of fashion-conscious recreational athletes, the attention to detail of the Italian or the restlessness of the Swabian soul, they all breathed a joie de vivre into the new smart. This was the quality that gave this innovative automobile a soul.

1996: show cars for Atlanta and Paris

At the 1996 Atlanta Olympics, the smart seemed almost close enough to grasp. At the world games, MCC presented a show car which already exhibited the silhouette of the production model, and with details such as the double-elliptical headlights which even foreshadowed elements of later models. This particular smart provided an unusually generous view of its interior, for the designers had done away with the doors in order to underscore for viewers the size of the interior provided by such a small footprint.

The show car presented at the Paris Auto Salon in September 1996 was a further development of the Atlanta study. Similarly open, this show car demonstrated, for the first time, a color distinction between the tridion safety cell (in silver) and the body panels (copper). This styling element would later become a point of recognition for the production model.

[3]

1997: Daimler-Benz takes over MCC AG

As vehicle development and planning of the manufacturing facilities entered an advanced stage, capital investments became necessary which exceeded Nicolas Hayek's resources and willingness to invest. Hayek probed Mercedes' inclination to take over a larger share of MCC AG. At the following management meeting in Biel, the Stuttgart team presented their partner with a buyout offer. In mid-February, Hayek accepted, and relinquished all of his shares.

The smart was officially presented in September, at the Frankfurt International Automobile Show. Just weeks later, on October 27, 1997, the first preproduction car rolled off the assembly line. Production of the three-cylinder engine for the smart city coupe had already begun in June 1997, in Berlin-Marienfelde.

In 1998, Daimler-Benz AG took complete control of Micro Compact Car AG; thenceforth the business would be called Micro Compact Car smart GmbH. In 2002, within the framework of a new smart model offensive, it was decided to give the first two models new names, and the business was also renamed, to smart GmbH.

smart
BB FY 217

Jürgen Zöllter

1.5 THE USA IN SIX DAYS: LAREDO TO BEMIDJI

- Testing the smart in the USA
- The innovative vehicle encounters broadminded acceptance
- "No journey too far for a smart"

Even during development and testing of the first-generation fortwo, consideration of the American continent had played a decisive role. Development of the eventual smart city coupe included extended test drives. Automotive journalist Jürgen Zöllter accompanied the smart on its long-distance trek across the USA. In six days from Texas to just shy of the Canadian border, test drivers became familiar not only with the compact car's qualities, but also the fascination with the smart engendered among the public, in town or country. Zöllter writes:

"Sluggishly, the river flows, dirty brown and full of trash. I had imagined the Rio Grande differently. It separates Nuevo Laredo from Laredo, homes from feedlots, Mexicans from Americans, rich from poor. South Texas with a view of Mexico: our hotel is near the bridge across the river that marks the border. Daily commuters flow into Texas from Mexico; a truck convoy pushes its way outward. It is five in the morning, and an oppressive humidity settles onto the human spirit.

An hour and a half later, a roll-up door is opened, on a prefabricated building graced by a solitary palm tree at one corner. Standing alongside is Rick, who checks our credentials. "OK, you can go in." Inside, workshops and offices, a telephone for the hotline to Renningen, Germany. John, formerly with Mercedes-Benz of North America, holds sway here. And then the smarts: six city coupes are lined up in rank and file, washed clean and fully fueled, two-way radios have been installed, the support truck has been loaded, Wolfgang takes his place in the lead car. At 8 AM, we get under way, leave the proving grounds and get onto northbound Interstate 35. One of the most difficult tests for the smart has begun. Our destination is Bemidji, Minnesota, far north near the Canadian border, exactly 3786 kilometers (2353 miles) away. Estimated driving time: five days, ten hours and seventeen minutes. Calculated fuel costs per smart: 81.73 Deutschmarks. The object of this test: to endure.

Six smarts, lined up like pearls on a string, purr between the lead minivan and trailing support truck, and soon leave the Interstate for northbound US 83, toward Carrizo Springs. Two engineers ride in each test car, taking regular turns at the wheel, listening as their smart talks to them, experience its reactions and document them. "A fine job," say the staybehinds. "A road trip through the entire breadth of America. Magnificent!" Then, the truck appears in the rear-view mirror, powerful and

threatening. Why don't we just give it more gas?

Wolfgang in the lead car is our scout and team leader, all in one. He sets the pace, and regularly gets on the radio to ask about engine rpms, water and oil temperatures. What are the turbocharger inlet and outlet temperatures? The co-drivers read off the data, a notebook PC perched on their knees. Bernd records it all, in his own PC, the team's central computer.

Until noon, the landscape remains flat, covered by a stubborn fog. We pass huge fields with hundreds of oil wells, rising up and down like giant hammers on the oilfields. Steady and leisurely, as if there is nothing else in the world but Texas and oil. Between them grow Texas steaks, on the hoof, on the sparse soil. Our journey goes westward, upstream along the Rio Grande. In Del Rio, we shut down our engines at a gas station out in the Texas desert. The crews have not yet gotten out, and already it starts. "What are those little things?" asks the gas station attendant. In minutes, we are surrounded by American cars; the curious get out and forget to shut down their engines or air conditioning systems. They ask if we came over from Germany with these cars, where we're headed, and why, for that matter. The fact that the smart is not an electric car for California city traffic has to sink in. Finally, the question: "Where is the engine?"

Here, we get the first lesson of our smart test drive: Americans are open to any new idea that amazes them. The fact that the smart engine gets by with just three cylinders and a displacement of only 0.6 liters is met with speechlessness. The fact that it can mobilize 55 horsepower, and get up to 81 miles per hour or 140 km/h, elicits amazement. The revelation that a smart will cover more than 40 miles on a single gallon of fuel is greeted by applause. By American standards, "incredible."

Three hours later, all of us swear that if we ever again pass through Sanderson, Texas, on Route 90, we will not stop to sample its food; steaks turned to charcoal and concrete-hard French fries served on tables sticky with spilled cola should be experienced only once per lifetime. With full stomachs (and our throats doing their best to keep it down), we continue toward Fort Stockton. Just outside town, where US 285 meets Interstate 10, we encounter a sheriff coming the other way. He executes an elegant, sweeping U-turn and stops the last smart in the convoy. What are all these cars about, he wants to know. Germans? He was in Germany once, visiting relatives. What town? Stockholm, he thinks. He doesn't remember exactly anymore. But for all that, he knows the way to our hotel. The first day is behind us, and at the evening debriefing, the following observations are recorded:

Had lots of fun, awakened curiosity in people, often drove the Smart at full throttle across the Texas plains, towards evening encountered the foothills of the Sierra Madre, up to 1020 meters (3346 feet) above sea level. Nothing abnormal to note about the test cars, which have been fitted with different pedal modules. The ABS brake setups also differ from one another. We duly record the effects of these differences.

On the second day, we get a 5:30 wake-up call. After a rather sparse "Breakfast De Luxe," the day can only get better. We swap cars among us. Today, every team of two will drive the car that had been driven by the following team on the previous day; other drivers, other impressions. Nothing, no observation, no nuance, must escape the test team.

At 7 AM, we're back on US 285. The smart engines purr like clockwork, and propel us through a gently rising landscape. At noon, we stop at Roswell, the world UFO capital in New Mexico, and park directly in front of the museum. Those who, based on recent dining experiences, have decided to go on a diet today, attach themselves to the museum guide to visit aliens, UFOs, and other oddities. Dieter and Gunter stand guard to protect the smart squadron against alien abduction. Wolfgang befriends the captain of a land yacht who, after a test-sitting, absolutely wants to buy a smart. But, how, or better said, where?

The smart city coupe is a car for Europe, for everyday service in the streets of Naples, Copenhagen or Lisbon. The newly formed automobile manufacturer MCC (Micro Compact Car AG) has only sent the two-seater overseas to ensure that it is ready for series production: once for winter testing in New Zealand and to Norway's North Cape, and once to experience city traffic in Barcelona and Chicago. This time, the journey stretches from summer to winter in the space of six days. Wolfgang tries to explain to the American technology fan in Roswell that only the USA offers the ability to experience all possible climate extremes in the shortest possible time span: hot deserts, humid plains, high mountains, cold, wet swamps and extreme cold. And his partner in conversation is speechless. Several times, he paces off the length of the smart's flanks; he can hardly believe it. "Only eight feet long? Incredible!" Then he suddenly lies down, and peers under the smart, then sits in the passenger seat, displaced slightly rearward, and comments: "More freedom of motion than in my Town Car, which is twice as long. Ingenious!"

The smarts break into the everyday American automotive world like harbingers of a completely new age. Mighty Rambo-inspired off-road pickups, so-called "full-size trucks," slam on their brakes. The nature boy under the cowboy hat has to convince himself: "Are those really steered by people, or are they remote controlled?"

US Route 60 is edged with snow. We reach an altitude of 2235 meters (7333 feet) above sea level; a Santa Fe freight train has been pacing us for the past half hour. I have just counted off the 112th car behind four powerful diesel engines when Bernd calls on the radio for a reading of turbocharger boost pressure. Then we head for the fuel pumps again, and the test forms are duly filled in: tire pressure, tread wear, rock chips in the windshields are counted. There is hardly a parameter that isn't logged. And, at the evening team debriefing in Moriarty, New Mexico, the topic of discussion is whether the climate inside every smart was comfortable, whether heat was evenly distributed, whether the windshield wiper swept area was large enough. Where does wind noise enter the cabin? How comfortable is pedal pressure on long stretches? We fall into our beds, dead tired, at 9 PM. Anyone who cared to glance at the heavy, blue-gray cloud cover over the Rocky Mountains would have been certain that the next morning would bring snow.

But on the third day, as the high plains of Colorado roll under our wheels, the feared snow storms are mercifully absent. The thermometer drops to far below freezing, but the road remains dry. In the cozy warmth of our heated smart cockpits, musical suggestions are traded back and forth. The rock station at 101.5 is a clear favorite. Then Wolfgang reminds us to maintain radio discipline. A checklist for the upcoming cold weather function test is drawn up, by radio, of course. So we combine the utilitarian with the enjoyable.

In this way, the endless stretches of road lose their monotony. Darkness catches us in Colorado Springs. Finally, we see the lights of Castle Rock.

The next day, we take the measure of Wyoming. It is the Day of the Electronics Technicians. Last night, they had faxed our test data readouts to Renningen. This morning, the returned evaluation awaited them. With the help of their laptops, modifications were made to the smart electronics; the results are read out while we're underway, compared, and constantly discussed. Important parameters for series production are gleaned from every one of the smart practical evaluations. As a basis for quality evaluation, they are also sent to the system partners – the suppliers and subcontractors. As we reach our quarters late in the evening, the windows freeze over in short order. The name of this burg, just shy of the South Dakota border, is Gillette. It is home to gas stations, motels, and Rosie, who, filled with enthusiasm for our "wonder cars," throws the biggest steaks she can find into the frying pans for us.

The final stage is nearly 1000 kilometers – 600 miles – and none of us is really looking forward to the end. For what awaits us in Bemidji, Minnesota, is more or less monotonous days of testing on ice and snow. So Wolfgang accedes to the whishes of the test team's rock music section and permits a detour to Mount Rushmore. In the parking lot, under the gaze of American Presidents Washington, Jefferson, Lincoln and Roosevelt, we fill up our windshield washers, check the wiper blades, and reflect on the rock group Deep Purple, who once sent their own take on the iconic Presidential portraits around the world, as cover art for their album "Deep Purple in Rock." Which made this site as famous as the actual workplace of Presidents, the White House in Washington, had always been. We pen "Eight smarts were here" in the guest book, shoot a souvenir photo, and, with that, close the tourism chapter of our journey. For the next two hours, we head north. The mercury drops lower with every mile. We drive straight into the North American continental winter.

For six hours, we pass through the most monotonous region of the USA. Between Dickinson and Detroit Lakes, North Dakota, Interstate 94 runs almost arrow-straight for nearly 550 kilometers – 340 miles. The smarts purr through nearly Arctic cold. The only break in the monotony is our routine reporting of data by radio to the lead car, carrying Wolfgang and Bernd. The smarts track cleanly on freshly fallen snow, and make for good cheer. While the minivan out front, and the support truck following behind, are already at their traction limits, the smarts weasel their way through without problems. The thought of fitting winter tires never crosses our minds. Then, finally, the long-awaited off-ramp; we leave the Interstate and head into the home stretch, for Bemidji, Minnesota. Hardly a hundred kilometers (60 miles) from the Canadian border, most of the traffic in these parts consists of all-wheel-drive vehicles. Thirty degrees Celsius

below zero (-22 °F), and gas station attendant Bill, in Bemidji, is shoveling snow in his shirtsleeves. The next morning, we wash our smarts in his car wash. And he, too, has to take its measure: an eight-foot car that crosses the entire country in five days? They must be crazy, these Europeans – but somehow, the concept does strike him as ingenious. After all, with a smart in the garage, he'd finally have enough room for his snowmobile, his buggy and the motorbike.

So we end our test drive, secure in the knowledge that the smart city coupe fits as easily into the dense traffic of major European cities as in the big hearts of Americans. For five days, we put the smarts into the deep freeze of Bemidji. Then, we fill up again and drive back to Texas. For a smart, no destination is too far."

MC 210
MC 210

Jürgen Zöllter

1.6 SMARTVILLE: A TRAILBLAZING PRODUCTION CONCEPT IN HAMBACH

- Innovative manufacturing of an innovative vehicle
- The plant rises from a greenfield site
- Comprehensive environmental protection requirements are incorporated

"Critics of the smart project doubted that we could realize this innovative automobile in the space of only 2.5 meters, and equipped with such convincing safety technology. They had to learn, and today will recognize, that we are also treading completely new paths in production, to make this priceworthy car in a profitable manner." Jürgen Hubbert, at the time president of the management board of Micro Compact Car AG, said these words in 1997 at the opening of the smart plant in Hambach, France. And Harald Bölstler, then general director of MCC France SAS and first plant manager of the new production site, smartville, added "The smartville industrial park is more than just a new car plant. It is the result of a successful cooperation between MCC and its partners."

In this, not much has changed in the intervening years. Five system partners – Magna Chassis Systems, Magna Uniport, Plastal, Siemens VDO Automotive and ThyssenKrupp Automotive Systémes France – continue to deliver components directly to the assembly line in the factory, which is laid out in the shape of a giant plus sign. In some cases, they install their preassembled modules themselves in the smart. Time factors and flexibility, "just in time" methods and minimum delivery times on all levels are among the factors which remain exemplary today. The manufacturing site permits reduction in transportation and logistics costs to a minimum; even ten years ago, this allowed the smart city coupe (renamed the smart fortwo in 2003) to be assembled in less than five hours.

On September 14, 1994, a group of experts in search of a site for an industrial project in the automotive sector arrived in Hambach. Four days

[1]

later, the Europôle de Sarreguemines industrial district was presented to MCC management. The following steps proceeded with amazing smoothness. MCC's wishes for special infrastructure connections, including electricity, gas, and water supply, were met with minimal bureaucracy. In particular, MCC planners placed high value on all administrative bodies' respect for deadlines.

On December 7, 1994, Micro Compact Car AG, founded in the previous year, and the local French government responsible for Hambach, in the province of Lorraine, signed a letter of intent to secure the selected factory site. On December 20, 1994, this memorandum of understanding was followed by a contract between both partners. In record time, a production system arose in Hambach, and with it an automobile plant that drew worldwide attention.

The decision for Hambach was reached after careful consideration of more than 70 possible sites, and served as an affirmation of Europe as a manufacturing location. Centrally located in Europe, and in immediate proximity to the German border, smartville is connected to international traffic routes. It lies along the A4 autoroute between Strasbourg and Paris, and along a major rail line. In addition, the Sarreguemines region offers a great potential of qualified workers, who are often bilingual. Hambach permits flexible work schedules. France's lower labor rates compared to Germany or Switzerland were by no means the deciding factor for choosing this location. It was helpful that Lorraine, whose economy was undergoing extensive restructuring, made great effort to attract new industries. Finally, Hambach is located in France's structurally endangered coal mining region.

[2]

A tightly networked industrial complex

The greatest challenge for Hambach as a factory site was set by the Mercedes-Benz planning team, in their requirement for development of a networked industrial complex. Like the end product itself, it, too, would need to be modular, to permit the most efficient implementation of production processes. After rejecting L- and U-shaped layouts for the assembly line, the engineers hit upon the idea of dividing the line into four subsections. These were joined at a common center, with an assembly line threaded through all of them like a string of pearls. And so, the idea of the "assembly plus" was born, permitting optimum satisfaction of various logistics and assembly requirements. In simplified form, the four branches are responsible for the following functions:

- cockpit installation and undercar technical work,
  including drivetrain integration
- technical work on floorpan
- interior trim work
- exterior work

This plant layout takes up little space; maximum distances between loading dock and assembly line is ten meters. Furthermore, subsections of the line are independent of each other. In this way, small buffers can be provided, to avoid total shutdown of the line in the event of a fault.

An additional building functions as a product integration and preparation center (PZV, for "Produktintegrations- und Vorbereitungszentrum"). This is located outside the assembly complex, and forms the link between product development in Germany and the system

[1] smartville plant dedication, Hambach, 1997
Left to right: Flavio Cotti, Jacques Chirac, Helmut Kohl
[2] Aerial view of smartville

COMPONENT SYSTEMS WITHIN THE "SMART-PLUS" PRODUCTION SYSTEM

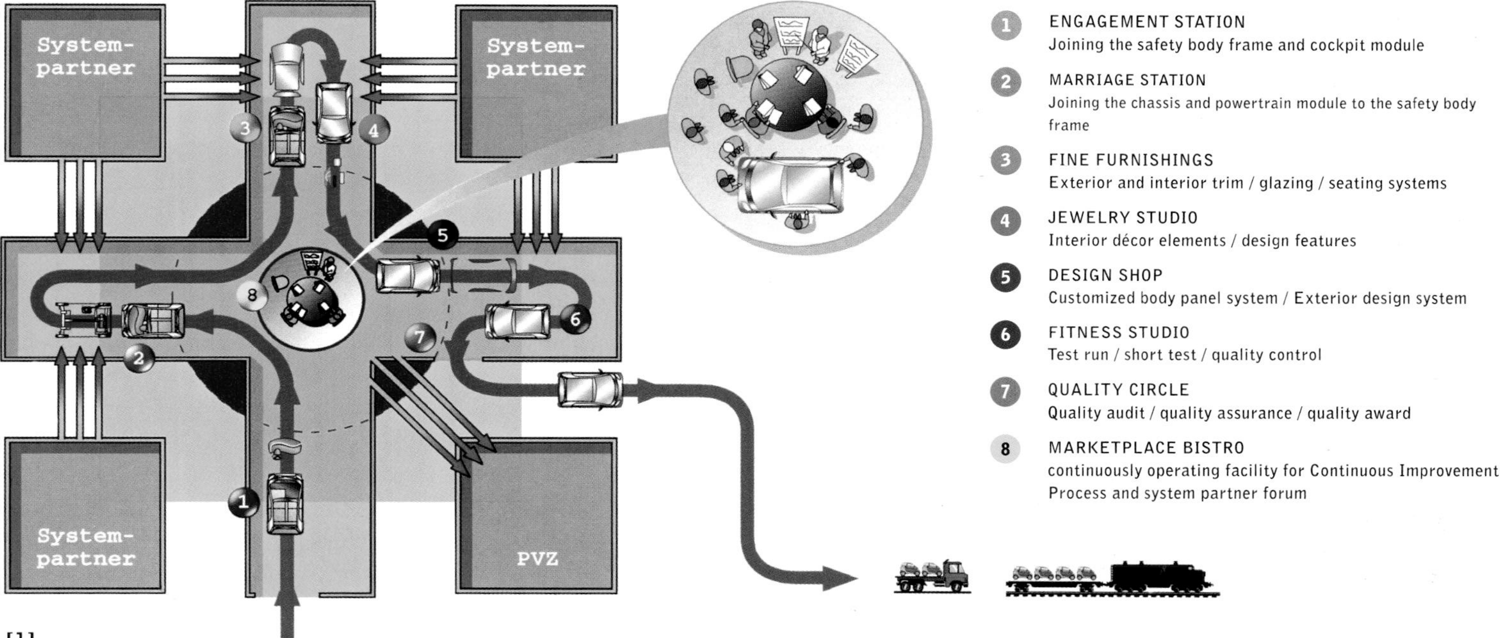

[1]

partners and assembly in Hambach. At the south end of the site, a test track permits evaluation of preproduction cars as well as ongoing quality assurance. In the space of 1.5 kilometers, various road surfaces are reproduced to facilitate suspension tuning. The smart Communications Center is located on an outlier of the site, adjoining the Autoroute A4. Its mission is to inform the public about the smart and smart culture. Moreover, it is available for conferences and symposia, as well as regional events.

Some numbers to characterize the networked operations in smartville: the small number of smart employees, only about 900, in all branches, indicates the high degree of external capacity utilization. If one counts the system partner employees, smartville employs about 1700 people.

The partnership model, a completely new development conceived in the mid-1990s for Hambach and the smart fortwo, is a further development of the conventional manufacturer/supplier relationship. It elevates the auto manufacturer to a position as a system integrator, a process manager and producer with holistic responsibility. On the other hand, each system partner is entrusted with sweeping responsibility.

Today, we know that such modern systems bring out extraordinarily motivated partners, who, through their own innovative efforts, contribute to economical implementation of joint goals.

The assembly process for the new smart fortwo encompasses a total of 140 workstations, which are traversed in just 3.5 hours. This represents an efficiency increase of about 20 percent, compared to the first smart generation, and is an absolute high for European manufacturers.

---

[1] "smart plus" factory concept

Closely joined system partners

The competitiveness of the joint project was to be strengthened through the synergies of know-how and creativity of all participating partners – in 1994, that was the initial position for MCC's cooperation with its system partners. Since then, this has developed into the "smart alliance," with its highly regarded "code of cooperation." This underscores the shared responsibility and mutual goals of all five system partners working at Hambach.

Magna Chassis Systems produces the smart's tridion safety cell. Siemens VDO Automotive is responsible for the cockpit module, including its installation. ThyssenKrupp Automotive Systémes France assembles the rear axle and final drive module on site. Plastal produces the body panels as well as other exterior trim, on site. And Magna Uniport supplies doors and lid modules.

Also firmly integrated in the cooperative model, but not located in Hambach, are the system partners for smart's drivetrain and suspension. The three-cylinder turbodiesel engines and axles are sourced from the Daimler network: the engines from Kölleda, the axles from Hamburg. All gasoline engines for the new smart, developed jointly with Mitsubishi, are supplied by the Mitsubishi plant in Mizushima, Japan.

In this way, smart France builds the new smart fortwo with a total of only five system partners and eleven direct suppliers of subsystems.

Not only development and production of the smart broke new ground; logistics were built up in close cooperation with the operating organizations, who also located in smartville. Logistics and transportation operator Panopa is responsible for supplying parts to the assembly line, sourcing parts and accessories, and controlling transportation modes. Freight forwarder Mosolf is the partner responsible for delivering finished customer vehicles.

Between 1998 and 2006, a grand total of 700,256 units of the first smart generation, both coupes and cabrios, left the smartville industrial park. The faultless quality of the delivered vehicles is a measure of the functionality of the innovative partnership model and production system as practiced at Hambach. Its high degree of flexibility and adaptability was once again shown in preparing the site for the second product generation of the smart fortwo. The industrialization process for the new model was executed during 2006, with a high proportion of re-utilized facilities and without need for any temporary storage. The assembly line was interrupted for several weeks, in three phases, during assembly of the old model, to prepare for the new model. Pre-production examples of the second generation two-seater were built in Hambach during these conversion phases. January 2, 2007, marked SOP – start of production – for the Model 451, the new smart fortwo, in smartville.

Environmental protection: written large

All phases of the product life cycle, beginning with development of individual smart components, through building the factory park in Hambach, to the product utilization and recycling phases, were and remain integrated within a strict ecological concept. The factory park in Hambach realized an unmatched model of ecological responsibility. All buildings are free of formaldehyde and hydro-fluorocarbons. The façades are clad in "Trespa," a raw material derived largely from easily replenished European wood. Distinction is even made between drainage from gutters, and that from roads and parking lots: roof drainage is used in storage ponds for firefighting use. All other surface water is directed through oil separators, treated in storage basins, and then re-utilized.

A central biological water treatment plant, reflecting the highest state of the art, treats all sanitation and industrial wastewater. The plant uses biological membranes and the Biosep process, a highly flexible recycling system first employed in France. The cleaned, treated wastewater is used to irrigate the landscaped grounds, and for cooling purposes in the production process.

The innovative paint shop, the world's first volume-production powder painting facility, contributes to environmental protection. In this facility, the chassis of the two-seat smart is completely powder coated. This economical and environmentally friendly coating process was first applied to automobile manufacturing in this plant, in 1997. Beyond its especially high degree of environmental responsibility, the process

Exhaust air filtration facility

is marked by the high level of coating quality it provides. Also, no solvents are emitted, and no hazardous waste such as paint sludge is generated. Moreover, the entire process employs unpassivated zinc phosphate treatment, in other words, free of lead and cadmium. Strict implementation of ecological targets is also apparent in recapture and re-use of excess material, such as overspray powder.

In implementing the smartville energy concept in Hambach, Lorraine, energy conservation policy was given high priority from the very beginning, starting with effective noise and thermal insulation of the building façades, to the consistent implementation of holistic thermal recapture concepts. For example, waste heat from die casting operations and vented air from the paint shop is directed over rotating heat recovery units and thermal wheels. Waste heat reutilization, unique on this scale, eliminates the need for cooling towers, and thereby reduces costs as well as use of resources. The smartville utilities installation, consisting of a heating plant and a power generation facility, employs the latest technological insights. Merely the combustion of natural gas in place of conventional fuels has resulted in lower pollutant emissions. Utilization of waste heat results in increased efficiency.

Harmonic integration of the factory park in the gently rolling green hills of Lorraine ensures the viability of an ecological revegetation concept. Its most significant characteristic is the flowing transition of the factory grounds into the adjoining village and forest landscape. The revegetation concept includes planting of meadows and tree-lined avenues, but also fruit gardens. Along with the firefighting basin, a pond, similarly equipped with “Biotop” equipment, is stocked with water plants and green vegetation to provide ecological balance.

From the beginning, environmental protection efforts were a firmly entrenched component of smart development. These are documented by an environmental management system certified according to DIN EN ISO 14001. So-called monomaterial systems result in the smart’s exemplary recyclability, and provide an impressive complement to its innovation potential.

In addition, the modular construction of the smart guarantees the ability for economical dismantling at the end of its life cycle. This is a precondition for closed material cycles. With its dynamic, continuously improved environmental management system, the smart marque has established a benchmark for environmentally responsible, individual mobility.

Jürgen Zöllter

1.7 DESIGN: BETWEEN INDIVIDUALITY, INNOVATION AND ART

- First studies probe the limits
- The production car incorporates the inspiration of preceding studies
- The smart as an objet d'art

[2]

Ever since the first models of the city coupe were developed, the smart marque has always taken the road less traveled. The concept is, above all, characterized by a daring design which self-consciously turns engineering details such as the tridion safety cell into a component of the overall automobile concept.

The studies which prepared the way for the smart city coupe probed the limits; first, there was the stark, strictly utilitarian NAFA of 1981, which placed function ahead of all formal aesthetics. At that point in time, such a clearly drawn car was the correct choice, since the new microcar concept still had to be delineated.

The California experiments of the early 1990s, by contrast, came off as trendy, colorful. Alongside technical innovation, they placed high emphasis on exploring the aesthetic possibilities of this new vehicle class. And again, the pronounced experiment with form and color represented an important step toward the production version.

Ultimately, the smart city coupe incorporated all of these inspirations of its predecessors, amplified by numerous new developments and shapes. The

[3]

[4]

Left page Alberto Bertolin
[2] smart advertisement, MoMA
[3] The smart in the Museum of Modern Art (MoMA)
[4] The smart designed by Katherina Sieverding's master class

resulting vehicle set its own tone, and caused a sensation in the automotive world. Its appearance is perhaps best compared to that of the original Mini: a unique style and fashionable self-consciousness accompanied the premiere of both models, each of which made the small car format socially acceptable as well as roadworthy. The smart, however, placed even greater emphasis on the minimalist maxim than Sir Alec Issigonis' legendary design.

smart remained true to the design virtues of the first model, even in succeeding designs. This is particularly true of the manifold derivative models based on the original platform: even at first glance, cabrio, roadster and roadster-coupe are just as recognizable as smart vehicles, as are special models (crossblade) and studies (crosstown). smart is not only the youngest automobile marque, but has also become the signet of a new automotive awareness. And, despite technical differences with other models, this was underscored by the smart forfour.

The smart design was recognized by many different art projects. So, for example, after the production ended in late fall of 2006, the master class of renown artist Katharina Sieverding envisaged the second to last first-generation smart fortwo ever built as, literally, a glowing example of the automotive future. Presented in January 2007, in the hands of visual artists, the car, with its luminescent special paintwork, became a futuristic light source. The smart forfour, too, became an object of artistic expression; in 2006, a total of twenty individual forfour-based interpretations were created.

Probably its greatest success in the art world was celebrated by the smart city coupe as early as 2002. In that year, New York's Museum of Modern Art (MoMA) adopted it into its permanent collection. Previously, this honor had been bestowed on only five other automobile designs: VW Beetle, Willys Jeep, Jaguar E-Type, Cisitalia GT and a Ferrari Type 641/2 Formula 1 race car. Among this company, the smart is the first vehicle to be taken up in the famous museum's collection while it was still in production.

smart special editions by Jean-Charles de Castelbajac

[1]

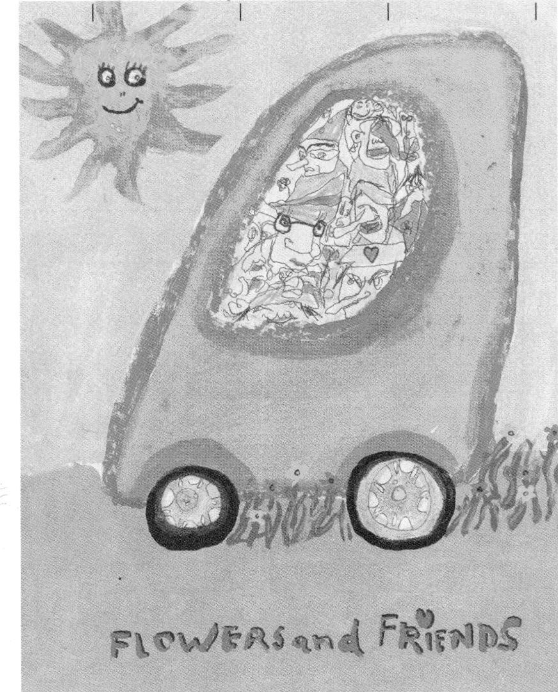

[2]

[3]

[4]

nojo®

[1] [2] [3] Patrik Farzar (sign reads "Great cars, top quality")
[4] Boris Hoppek

Why not Associates / Patrick Morrissey

Lucy McLauchlan

Jim Avignon

Richard Fenwick

Fork Unstable Media Ost / David Lindermann

Play / Marius Watz and Erik Johan Worsøe Eriksen

Artoo/Henrik Kürschner

Marok/Thomas Marecki

Die Gestalten/Sascha Minde

DAG

Horst Libera

Michael Zöllner

Campaign for 2001 Frankfurt International Auto Show (IAA)

Jürgen Zöllter

1.8 MODEL HISTORY: A SMART FAMILY

- The smart is constantly refined
- Additional models enrich the marque
- High-performance versions are built with BRABUS know-how

1998: smart city coupé

This vehicle was the ancestor of the smart idea, turned into reality, and became an automotive style icon. Twenty-six years after Johann Tomforde's first idea, the smart city coupe began rolling off the assembly line. Its dimensions remained astonishingly small: overall length 2.5 meters, 1.51 meters wide, and 1.52 meters tall. Thanks to its refined design, the smart imparted a dynamic, youthful impression.

Its body structure and engineering details underscored how thoroughly its developers had broken with traditional automotive concepts. The engine, a three-cylinder gasoline unit of only 598 cc, was located at the rear of the car. The tridion safety cell provided con-vincing crash safety, was responsible for smart's high level of stability, and, in conjunction with effective front and rear crush zones and modern restraint systems, provided passive safety on the level of much larger sedans. The second body element was the body panels themselves, in a color contrasting with that of the safety cell itself.

The city coupe was offered in trim levels named "pure," "pulse," and "passion;" the turbocharged engines

[1]

[2]

[1] The smart city coupé establishes a new dimension in individual transportation
[2] The body panel systems makes a colour change possible in less than two hours

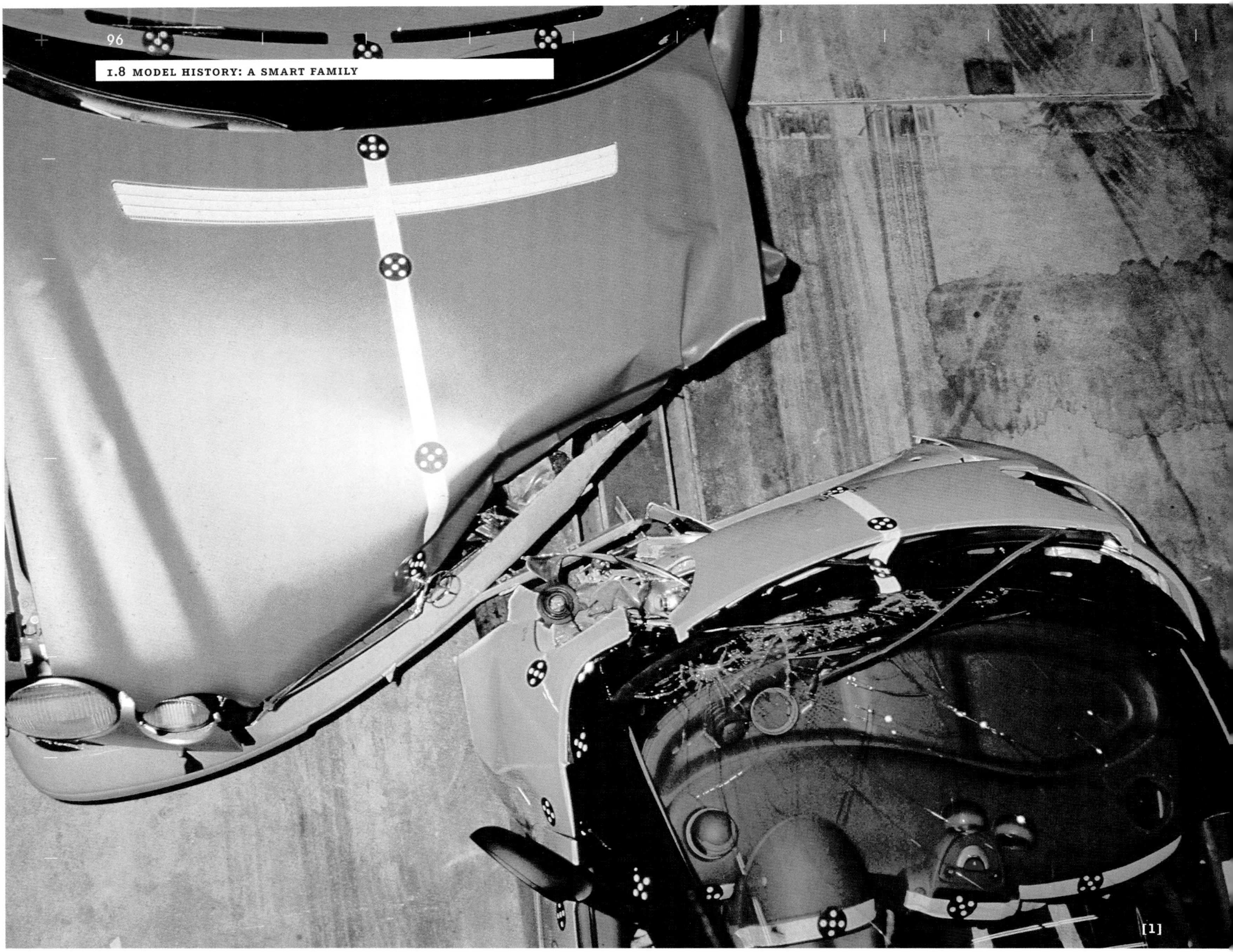

[1]

[2]

achieved outputs of 45 hp (33 kW), 55 hp (40 kW), and 61 hp (45 kW) respectively. The engineers achieved these successively higher power levels from the same engine displacement by increasing turbocharger boost pressure, to a maximum of 1.0 bar in the 61 hp (45 kW) smart pulse. This provided a maximum torque of 88 Newton-meters across an engine speed band from 2250 to 4500 rpm.

The smart passion delivered slightly less performance, with 55 hp (40 kW). This trim level, however, included a sunroof, tinted glass, starline design alloy wheels and bicolor taillights, a softouch automatic transmission, air conditioning with external temperature indicator, leather-wrapped steering wheel and shift knob.

Standard equipment for all smart variations included the "trust plus" vehicle dynamics control, derived from the ESP® electronic stability program; anti-lock brake system (ABS); electronic brake distribution (EBD); full-size airbags for driver and passenger; integral safety seats, belt tensioners and belt tension limiters, as well as pre-installed mounting points for quick installation of child safety seats.

[3]

The "trust plus" vehicle dynamics control derived its name from "Traktions- und Stabilitätskontrolle." The system's task was to avoid critical driving situations. To this end, ABS sensors and a transverse acceleration sensor continuously monitored the smart's driving situation.
In the event of excessive transverse acceleration, trust plus automatically reduced the throttle opening; if oversteer was detected, the clutch was disengaged.

As early as its market introduction in October 1998, the smart city coupe was also offered as a limited edition model, the limited/1, with a production run of 7500 examples. This variation included seats, door pockets, steering wheel and shift knob covered in light-colored leather. At their introduction, special limited/1 badging and their sequential vehicle serial numbers distinguished these special models from the regular production cars.

Early on, smart demonstrated the multiple possibilities for placing the city

[1] Crash test versus a Mercedes Benz E-Class
[2] Rollover crash test
[3] Special edition smart limited/1

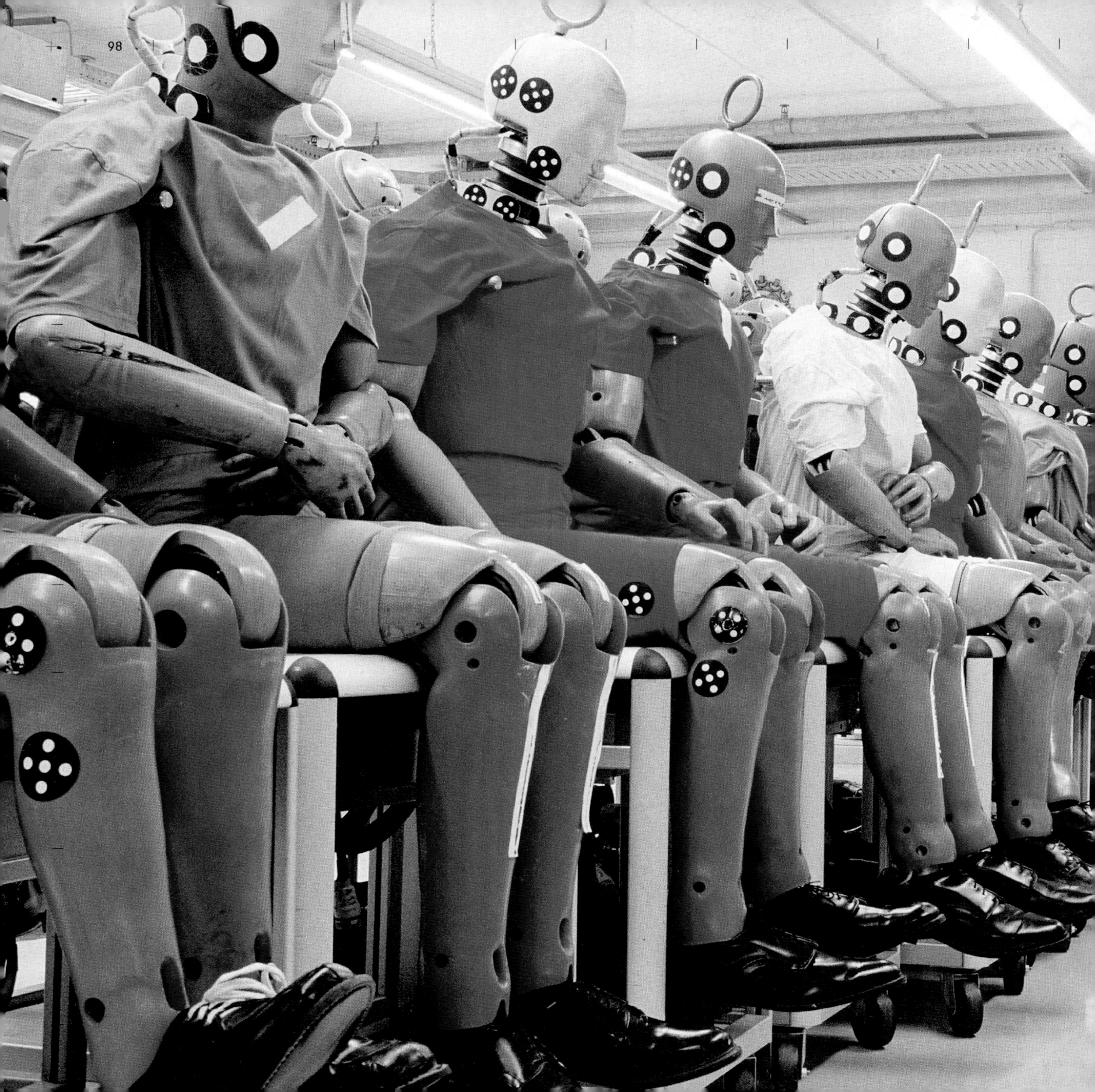

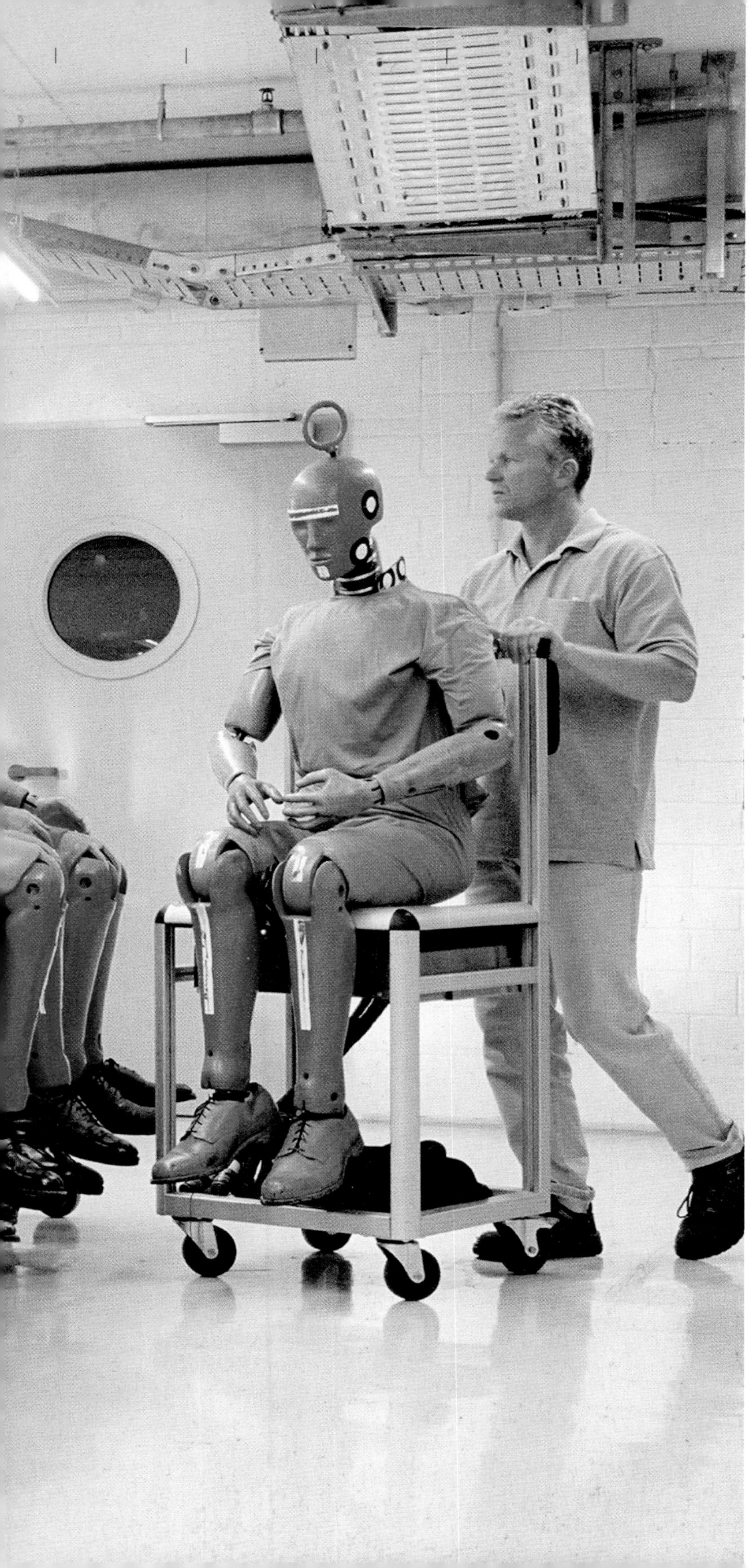

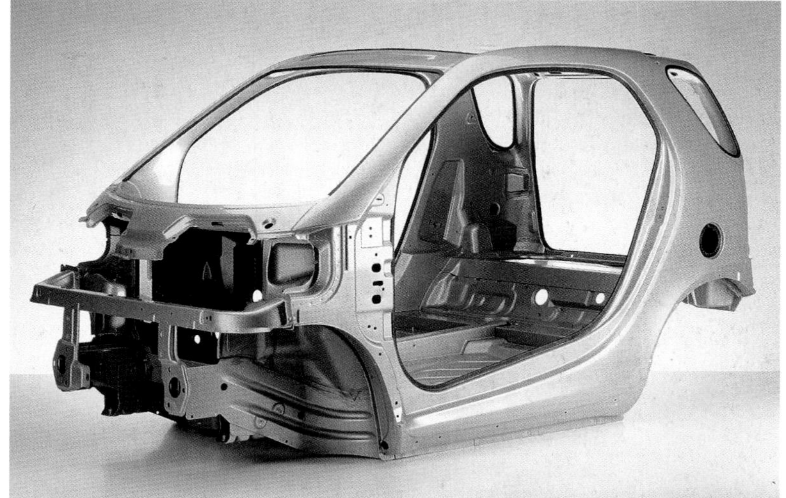

coupe into service for various special tasks. There were special versions for airport security, police, and fire departments. In 1998, Mercedes-Benz' own fire brigate placed an appropriately equipped vehicle into service at its Sindelfingen factory as a speedy communications vehicle and command post. The red car was fitted with siren and flashing blue emergency lights; the interior housed telephone, radio equipment, and a fire extinguishers.

Sales of the smart city coupe began in 1998 in Germany, Belgium, France, Italy, Luxembourg, Holland, Austria, Switzerland, and Spain. By 2007, smart was represented worldwide in 37 different countries. With the second generation of the smart fortwo, the marque will enter the American market as well.

Left: crash test dummies
Top: tridion safety cell

smart
Engineered by
Mercedes-Benz

1999: smart city coupé cdi

Direct-injection diesel technology found its way into the smart in 1999. The three-cylinder diesel engine displaced 799 cc and produced 41 hp (30 kW); it was the world's smallest volume-produced diesel automotive powerplant. Just like more powerful Mercedes-Benz engines, it was fitted with common rail direct injection, which provided levels of torque and low emissions previously unachievable in the diesel segment.

The smart cdi had an average fuel consumption of only 3.4 liters of diesel per 100 kilometers (according to NEFZ standards) – 69 U.S. miles per gallon, making the self-igniter a genuine „three liter" car. The ecologically exemplary diesel was the first variant offered by smart in North America; in 2004, it celebrated its Canadian debut. In its first year of sales, 4000 Canadian buyers opted for the economical car. Marcus Breitschwerdt, president of Mercedes-Benz Canada, summed it up: *"The smart fortwo is 'cool,' and Canadians love this car."* The cdi proved itself even in harsh Canadian winters, not least thanks to its electronic stability program, standard equipment since 2003.

Left: diesel engine with common rail direct injection technology

smart city cabrio tridion safety cell

2000: smart cabrio

In 1999, the heavens opened up for smart, as the marque presented a cabriolet based on the city coupe. This convertible met with great acclaim; this body variant captured perfectly the youthful, unconventional character of the smart idea. The lovable little car rolled out onto the roads in the spring of 2000. The cabrio had the identical compact dimensions as the city coupe, and, at 740 kilograms (1630 pounds), was just 10 kg (22 lbs.) heavier than the solid-roof version. The airy smart was available with the two larger gasoline engines and the diesel powerplant.

For the smart cabrio, innovative design of the convertible top permitted three variations on the theme of open motoring. At the touch of a button, the electrically actuated folding top could be rolled back to any desired position. Moreover, with a few quick manual operations, the electrically locked rear section could be lowered. Finally, the roof siderails could be removed and stowed in a special bin on the underside of the trunk lid. An even greater open-air experience was provided by a special model, introduced to the market in 2002: the smart crossblade.

BB F 5777

BB F 6957

BB F 8360

2002: smart crossblade

It would hardly be possible to have any more freedom. The smart crossblade had no doors, no roof, and no windshield. Its driver moved freely through the landscape, under an open sky, experiencing the wind in his face, and enjoyed an incomparable driving experience. The only obstacle to the free flow of air was a narrow, tinted wind deflector above the dashboard. Instead of conventional doors, the crossblade had steel safety bars fitted at passenger shoulder level. Supported by a gas springs, these swung vertically to allow entrance or egress.

The first advertising campaign for the smart concentrated on the essentials: "reduce to the max." The smart crossblade cashed in on this even as a study, presented at the 2001 Geneva Auto Show. This radical interpretation of the smart idea received an overwhelmingly positive media response, and was greatly admired by show visitors. smart, therefore, resolved to bring to market a special limited series of 2000 examples derived from the regular production model. In June 2002, the first customers took delivery of their individually numbered examples of the crossblade. Its minimalist equipment placed even greater emphasis on the tridion safety cell. In this smart model, the tridion design element was particularly noticeable. In the areas of the roll bar, B-pillars, and door sills, the safety cell was painted a matte titanium color. Black minimalist wheel covers underscored its dynamic appearance.

The entire interior of the smart crossblade was well armored against the effects of sun, wind, and weather. Instrument panel and seats were covered by a water-shedding, fire-engine-red synthetic material, contrasted by the black seatback inserts typical of this model. The interior floor was trimmed by a single-piece plastic tub; in the event of a downpour, four channels allowed water to drain out through the floor of the safety cell. Additionally, the tub protected electrical wiring against moisture. Each of the seating surfaces had two drain channels near the rearmost transverse seam. The driver airbag was protected by a waterproof hood. If necessary, the entire interior of the crossblade could be protected against sun and rain by means of an included tonneau cover. The black nylon cover could easily be stretched over the interior and held in place against the bodywork with sewn-in elastic straps.

The smart crossblade is an expression of personal freedom and independence; it is aimed at an exclusive customer base which places high value on personal independence. The open two-seater represents the smart brand's power of innovation. With regard to its standard installed safety technology, the special edition offered a level of protection comparable to the smart cabrio and smart city coupe; it was equipped with the now familiar restraint system of those models, with belt tensioners, belt tension limiters, and full-size airbags for driver and passenger.

The crossblade was powered by the familiar turbocharged engine of the city coupe and cabrio, with its power increased electronically to 70 hp (52 kW). Top speed was 135 km/h (84 mph); peak torque was 108 Newton-meters.

crossblade
cross europe
Mobil 1

crossblade
cross europe
crossblade
UKN 591
Mobil

2003: smart fortwo model development

A new, larger three-cylinder engine provided more power in the gasoline versions of the smart fortwo (previously badged as city coupé and cabrio). As of the 2003 model year facelift, the entry model was fitted with a 50 hp (37 kW) engine, while the more powerful smart produced 61 hp (45 kW) from an engine now displacing 698 cc. The new generation of gasoline engines met EU4 exhaust emissions standards. The proven cdi diesel engine of 41 hp (30 kW) remained unchanged.

Further innovations made the vehicles even more comfortable, safer, and more dynamic. The smart marque offered its customers as standard equipment technology normally only found in much higher vehicle classes; the former "trust plus" vehicle stability program was replaced by the ESP® electronic stability program, which added selective brake intervention to stabilize the vehicle. In addition, ESP® included further functions which made driving even more comfortable and safer, such as drive-off and braking assistants and anti-slip control. The ABS anti-lock brake system with its included EBV electronic brake distribution was integrated in the ESP® system. In addition, ESP® also permitted softer spring tuning and greater suspension travel than previously. No other car in the micro compact segment offered these features.

For added driving comfort and active safety in the automatic (softouch) mode, a kickdown function was introduced in production to allow rapid downshifts across one or two gears. In keeping with the uprated engines, shift sequences and gear ratios were optimized accordingly. Individual gears were now taller, and power development was noticeably more harmonious.

"As a result of our model development, smart city-coupé and smart cabrio customers will experience a completely new driving experience," said Philipp Schiemer, smart GmbH director of sales and marketing on the occasion of the 2003 model improvements. "We have concentrated on the 'intrinsic values' of the vehicles, and we succeeded in further improving an already extraordinary product."

Top: smart fortwo gasoline engine
Right: smart fortwo cabrio with unique "cubic printing." Unfortunately, not accepted by the marketplace, and therefore soon retired.

smart
BB F 5120

2003: smart fortwo BRABUS

Along with model improvements, 2003 saw the presentation of BRABUS versions, developed as a joint venture by smart and BRABUS GmbH. In 2002, smart and Bottrop (Germany) – based vehicle customizer BRABUS founded a joint venture under the name smart-BRABUS GmbH. In 2004, at a cost of 16 million Euros, the new company opened its headquarters in Bottrop: an ultramodern technology and competence center.

Introduced to the market in 2003, the smart city coupé BRABUS and smart cabrio BRABUS, (renamed in 2004 as smart fortwo BRABUS), extended the model line upward. These satisfied the highest customer demands for exclusivity, individuality, innovation and dynamics. Both top-of-the-line models were powered by a 75 hp (55 kW) engine which, in contrast to the regular production cars, permitted a top speed of 150 km/h (93 mph).

smart

BRABUS

2003: smart roadster and roadster-coupé

An especially intense driving experience was offered by two sports cars, the smart roadster and smart roadster-coupé, which entered the market in April 2003. Styling studies and show cars had already been presented in 1999 at the Frankfurt IAA, and in 2000 at the Paris Auto Show; the final body variations was presented in 2002. With these two vehicles, smart established a connection to the long-standing tradition of the pure, compact roadster that flowered in the 1950s and '60s. The bodywork of both smart sports cars differed at the rear; while the roadster had a notchback with fixed rear glazing, the roadster-coupé employed an all-glass hatchback.

For the roadster, displacement of the rear-mounted engine grew to 698 cc. The larger engine was also introduced on other smart models. In the roadster, the three-cylinder powerplant delivered either 61 hp (45 kW) or 82 hp (60 kW). The roadster-coupé was only available with the more powerful engine. With an overall length of just under 3.5 meters, a height of 1.2 meters, and curb weight of just 790 kg (1740 lbs.), top speeds of the roadsters were 160 km/h (99 mph) and 175 km/h (109 mph); the slightly heavier roadster-coupé could reach 180 km/h (112 mph).

These dynamic, agile smart two-seaters offered a unique driving experience, in which not only the destination but the journey itself was the reward. Their combination of direct handling, outstanding roadholding, and an astounding level of comfort made it possible to intensely experience a level of driving dynamics unmatched by any other compact car in their class. smart roadster and smart roadster-coupé were equipped with the ESP® vehicle dynamics system as standard equipment. The technology of both sports cars was based on the classical smart, which thenceforth, as both coupe and cabrio, was renamed the fortwo, in order to distinguish it from the new models. Market introduction of the smart roadster and smart roadster-coupé was the first decisive step toward expanding the smart product palette, and with it the marque itself.

With a roof system consisting of both soft and hard tops, which could be used together or alone, the roadster and roadster-coupé opened the way for their owners to enjoy the highest levels of open-air driving pleasure. Along with a two-piece removable composite roof, which could be stowed in the rear trunk, an electric folding top was available for the smart roadster as well as the roadster-coupé. This could be opened or closed at any speed up to the vehicle top speed – a unique ability within the entire market.

Soon, these were followed by BRABUS versions of the smart sports car. These smart-BRABUS GmbH developments celebrated their world premiere at the 2004 Geneva Auto Show. Both model variations were upgraded in terms of performance and equipment. They now developed 101 hp (74 kW); the roadster achieved a top speed of 190 km/h (118 mph), and the coupe 195 km/h (121 mph). These performance capabilities guaranteed even more driving fun. Standard equipment for the nimble two-seater included sport suspension, 17 inch wheels, softouch automatic shifter, black leather heated sport seats, and a three-spoke leather-covered steering wheel with shift paddles.

As a styling study, BRABUS even presented a smart roadster-coupé fitted with a twin-turbo V6 at the back instead of the stock three-cylinder. Its 1396 cc displacement motivated 170 hp (125 kW) and took less than six seconds to sprint to 100 km/h (62 mph).

At the end of 2005, after 43,000 examples, production of the smart roadster and roadster-coupé ceased. In two years of production, both sports cars based on the smart fortwo platform underscored the dynamism of this vehicle concept in a most convincing fashion.

2004: smart forfour

smart first deviated from the principle of a two-seater rear-engined car in 2004, as the 3.75 meter long, 1.70 meter tall forfour came to market. The sporty five-door had uncommon dimensions for the marque, and opened up a new, highly competitive market segment for smart. This newcomer in the small-car segment was initially offered in three different gasoline-engined variations. Three-cylinder engines, as found in the fortwo, were enlarged to 1124 cc and 75 hp (55 kW), as well as 1332 cc and 95 hp (70 kW). A 1499 cc four-cylinder developing 109 hp (80 kW) propelled the forfour1.5 liter. The engine lineup was rounded out by the top-of-the-line gasoline power-plant, installed in the smart forfour sportstyle: 1.5 liters, 122 hp (90 kW). Two three-cylinder diesels, each with 1493 cc, were offered: a 68 hp (50 kW) and a 95 hp (70 kW) version, available as of August 2004.

The smart forfour was bigger than any of the marque's previous models. Nevertheless, with a curb weight of less than 1000 kg (2200 lbs.), it still subscribed to the virtues of the smart idea. Its specific output was about 12.2 kg/kW (9 kg per hp, or 20 pounds per hp) and therefore represented the same attractive power-to-weight ratio as the smart roadster and roadster-coupé. Agile and safe handling were ensured by firm tuning of the "active drive" suspension and a well-balanced weight distribution with extremely short rear overhang.

The interior of the smart forfour made a convincing case, with a newly conceived lounge concept and the possibility of variable interior layouts. Folding the front seatbacks resulted in a large horizontal seating surface, at nearly the same level as the rear seats. In addition, the rear bench seat had a 150 mm (6 inch) range of adjustment. Folding armrests, additional supports and cushions transformed the interior into a living space.

The marque's characteristic tridion safety cell of hot-dip galvanized steel acted like an extremely rigid capsule to protect its occupants in the event of an accident. The smart forfour also included as standard equipment the ESP® electronic stability program for assured vehicle dynamics under all conditions and situations, plus full-size airbags for driver and passenger, and side air bags. All seating positions of the smart forfour employed three-point safety belts and headrests. Special child seats and restraint systems were available. The smart forfour initially appeared in two design and equipment levels: the sports-oriented "pulse" line and the more comfort-oriented "passion" line. Additionally, at the time of market introduction, a very attractively priced special edition, "blackbasic," was offered. This represented the basis for the future "pure" trim level, for which an additional 63 hp (47 kW) engine was added to the program. The pure variant was intended to make the smart forfour attractive to an especially price-conscious clientele.

smart also added to the other end of the forfour lineup. At the 2005 Geneva Auto Show, the marque presented the forfour BRABUS; with a top speed of 221 km/h (137 mph), it was the first production smart able to exceed 200 km/h (124 mph). The car was offered in two versions, the smart forfour BRABUS and forfour BRABUS Xclusive. The Xclusive variant differed in its especially luxurious interior trim. Both variants rolled on 17-inch wheels and were powered by a 177 hp (130 kW) four-cylinder turbocharged engine supplied by Mitsubishi and developed for use in the smart forfour by smart BRABUS GmbH in Bottrop, Germany.

Production of the four-seat smart ended in the summer of 2006, after about 100,000 were built. The last examples of the forfour included an individually styled special model, the smart forfour "for me." These carried a customer-selected name as a signature on the B-pillar.

BB F 9209

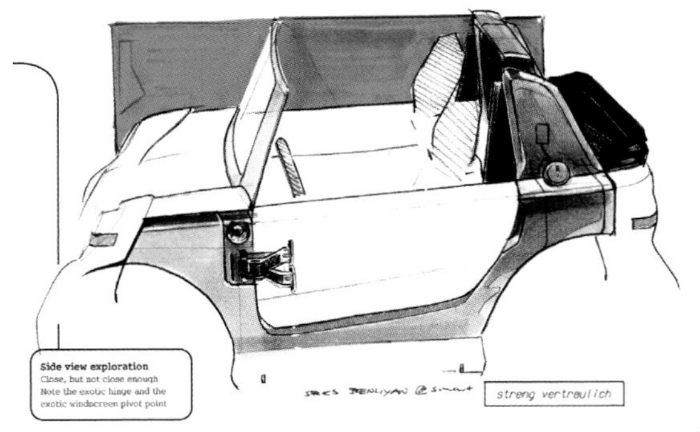

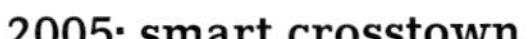

2005: smart crosstown

The smart "crosstown" show car, presented at the 2005 Frankfurt International Auto Show, combined gasoline and electric powerplants in a futuristic hybrid drive system. The smart crosstown was also shown at the 2006 Geneva salon. It demonstrated the potential available in the smart fortwo's unique concept. The open car, with its upright windshield, was, however, not intended for series production.

Also in 2005, within the framework of a technology forum, smart presented additional design studies with alternative drive systems. Along with a prototype all-electric smart fortwo ev, smart also showed prototypes of a natural gas powered smart fortwo as well as a micro hybrid and a cdi hybrid.

Instrument panel of the smart crosstown styling study, with PDA and USB memory sticks

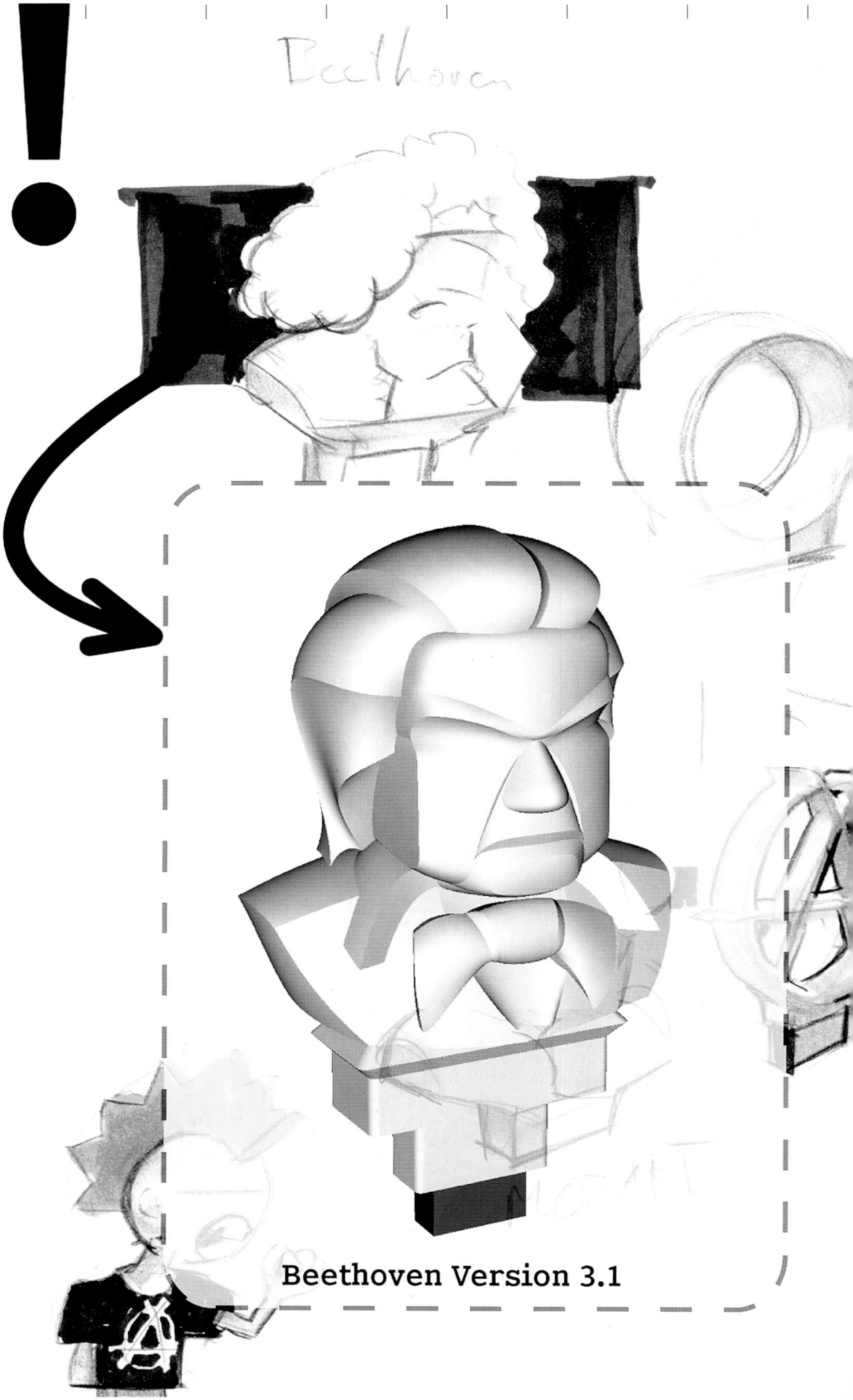

Beethoven

Beethoven Version 3.1

Vyvyan
Punk
Best OF
Heavy Metal
200K

[2]

[3

[4

2006: smart electric drive

In 2006, the Öko-Trend environmental research institute bestowed its "Auto Environment Certificate" on the environmentally friendly smart, in its 61 hp (45 kW) gasoline form. The researchers honored smart's holistic efforts toward ecologically responsible automobile production.

These efforts included a large-scale test in Great Britain using a fleet of electric smart fortwos. One hundred examples of the smart fortwo ed (electric drive) were offered to selected British customers as leasing cars. The smart fortwo ed celebrated its world premiere at London's British International Motor Show in the summer of 2006.

Propulsion was provided by a 41 hp (30 kW) electric motor. Operating costs per kilometer were appreciably lower than those of the already very economical gasoline-powered smart fortwo; while the latter managed a per-kilometer cost of about 0.06 Euros, already far ahead of its market competitors, the electric smart fortwo managed about 0.02 Euros per kilometer, making it especially interesting for customers in metropolitan London. The smart fortwo ed was classified as a "zero emissions vehicle," which made it exempt from the London congestion charge. This made the car an economical proposition for the customer, because the congestion charge savings financed the battery lease.

The smart fortwo ed offered attractive performance. Acceleration to 60 km/h (36 mph) was comparable to that of a gasoline-powered model; top speed was on the order of 120 km/h (75 mph). Energy consumption remained reasonable, at 12 kWh/100 km and a range of 110 km (68 miles). As the numbers suggest, the smart fortwo ed was a vehicle ideally suited to short-distance city driving conditions. Charging time to go from 30 percent to 80 percent of battery capacity was three and a half hours. Charging a completely drained battery took no more than eight hours, making overnight charging an attractive option. The charging connector was located under the "fuel filler" lid which normally housed the gasoline or diesel filler neck.

Installation of the electric propulsion unit was possible without excessive modifications. The motor was located at the rear, in the exact same position occupied by the normal combustion engine. The transmission, permanently locked in second gear, was also located in the same area. The smart fortwo ed therefore did not have the familiar shifter, but rather made do with just a forward and reverse gear.

The charge condition indicator was located in place of the engine tachometer, centrally located on the instrument panel along with the analog clock. Otherwise, nothing was changed; interior and trunk volume remained as before. Even the energy storage unit was unobtrusive, in the case of the smart fortwo ed either a zebra or nickel metal hydride battery, weighing 137 kg (301 lbs.) and centrally located under the floorpan.

[2] Electric motor
[3] Charging connector
[4] Battery charge condition indicator

A new smart fortwo test car, underway in the USA

BBQ

[1]

2007: To be continued: the second model generation – smart fortwo

It remains the most controversial car of our time. It is beloved and simultaneously misunderstood by auto enthusiasts, aesthetes, technology fans, and representatives of the automotive competition. It polarizes, exactly as smart's creatives intended. In that, the experts agree: the smart fortwo is the most daring attempt of the past ten years to couple humans' need for individual mobility and their sensibility for changing ecological limitations. In 2007, the shortest car of our time, equipped by the efforts of a most ingenious, competent team, continues on in its second model generation.

"With the new smart fortwo, the advantages of the first model generation undergo further development. Our new two-seater was refined in every automotive discipline," said smart development chief Dr. Klaus Badenhausen. The date was November 2005, the scene was the roof of a Stuttgart parking garage, the occasion the premiere of the new model. And Dr. Badenhausen was referring to the smart's new maturity in preparation for entering the American market. The new model would carry the success of the clever two-seater to the world's largest automotive market, the United States of America – with optimized economy of space, even greater driving safety, and allaround greater driving fun. According to Dr. Badenhausen, tuning a suspension for a wheelbase of only 1.86 meters was more difficult than the fine tuning of many an exclusive luxury sedan.

smart fans can rejoice! Compared to its predecessor, nuances of the new two-seater have been refined, yet it remains true to its concept and design. It carries the same high brow, and exceeds the overall length of its predecessor by a significant 19 cm. Its wheelbase has grown by six cm, yet its maneuverability and its unique ability to park sideways in conventional parallel parking spots have been retained. The interior, however, boasts a seven cm increase in legroom, and 70 liters more luggage space. Within the space 2.69 meters, the smart fortwo arrives on the scene as a city car that, with its two slightly staggered, first-class integral seats, imparts to its passengers an impression of spaciousness comparable to the front seats of a Mercedes-Benz C-Class. With (two stage) front and optional side air bags and once again improved crash structures, with ESP, ABS and brake assistant, it is a candidate for the title of "world's safest small car." Compared to the first smart generation, its dashboard shows more linearity, the "wave" is gone. This comes across as a bit more mature, and is a precondition for satisfying all international requirements for occupant protection. Large storage areas also permit young city dwellers in alternative cultural circles to carry along large quantities of consumables to ensure personal well-being. After all, smart's creators are well aware that the California customer likes to perform his or her morning routine inside the car, on the way to work. And so, the new smart fortwo goes west.

On the road, the new three-cylinder rear-mounted engine purrs along as ever, as unperturbed as a contented kittycat. This may surprise those who are aware of the completely new engine of the second-generation fortwo; it was developed in cooperation with Mitsubishi and exhibits the same smoothness as its predecessor, yet offers increased power output and more efficient use of fuel. From one liter of displacement, the engine develops the customer's choice of 61 or 71 hp, or, in the turbo version, a respectable 84 hp (45, 52, and 62 kW respectively). Development boss Dr. Badenhausen promises that the most powerful engine manages the sprint from zero to 120 km/h (75 mph) in nine seconds. A fortwo massaged by smart's house tuner BRABUS even manages 98 hp (72 kW) yet on average needs only 5.9 liters per 100 km (40 mpg). The most economical way to drive a smart fortwo is, as always, the 0.8 liter three-cylinder turbodiesel with common rail direct injection and open diesel particulate filter. Daimler makes this engine exclusively for the smart; thanks to this engine, customers of the smart fortwo cdi enjoy a "three liter" car with a remarkable level of environmental responsibility.

[2]

Engine output is apportioned by a semi-automatic five-speed gearbox, developed in cooperation with transmission specialist Getrag. Shift lag had always been a point of criticism on the first-generation smart; shifts are now satisfying quick, and thanks to addition of a second gear selector drum, the driver can now skip gears. Naturally, the transmission of the second-generation smart fortwo again provides a fully automatic mode. One especially pleasing feature is that the new two-seater does not exhibit any significant weight transfer effects, reacts spontaneously to throttle, and tracks through turns precisely. The steering reacts with greater sensitivity than in any other city car in its segment.

As a result of Daimler's restructuring of its small car marque in 2005 and 2006, the new fortwo emerged as an exclusive model. It demonstrates the viability of daring decisions when combined with long-range strategic planning – even if it did take some time to gain widespread acceptance. With care and innovative strengths, the new smart imparts the cult character of the original model with a new impulse. Its fans celebrate it as an expression of futuristic, responsible mobility. It wins over new customers with a personable demeanor, compelling appointments and a unique level of driving enjoyment.

The development potential contained within the new smart fortwo generation may be discerned from the announcement of a fortwo equipped with a micro-hybrid gasoline engine. With an eye to the North American market, development chief Dr. Klaus Badenhausen promises that this vehicle, equipped with a highly complex drivetrain management system, will cut highway fuel consumption by five percent, and city consumption by up to 15 percent. An indication of its acceptance in American cities may be gleaned from an encounter prior to the introduction of the first-generation smart two-seater. At a gas station, the driver of a full-size pickup truck gazed with fascination upon the gas pump next to the prototype micro car, and begged that such an efficient model car never be allowed to grow up: "Don't make it any bigger. It's already huge."

---

[1] The second model generation, with the special edition limited/1, the smart fortwo cabrio and coupé, at the 2007 Geneva Auto Show
[2] The two smart fortwo models, cabrio and coupé, by house tuner BRABUS

1.9 SMART IN THE PRESS

"More brain sweat has never before been invested in a small car, and it is undeniable that the Smart is part of the automotive future. It is an intelligent car, and not a makeshift proposition; it is not an expression of a lack of resources, but rather proof of a great deal of understanding. Its small size is not an accident, but rather deliberate, and we are looking forward to a warm summer with the Smart Cabrio... (regarding the smart fortwo cdi). Frankfurter Allgemeine Zeitung, April 4, 2000

CUTTING CO_2 DOESN'T HAVE TO BE EXPENSIVE

Result: a top ten list, where every gram of CO_2 below the self-imposed limit counts. The rankings derive from the cost per amount of CO2 reduction. Winner: the new Smart fortwo.
Focus, April 2, 2007

CELEBRITIES ARE CAPTIVATED: DAIMLER'S NEWEST MODEL

"The smart has simply gotten grandiose," says Professor Werner Mang as he contemplates the facelift of the so-called Fortwo. "No cosmetic surgeon could have managed it any better. And this was a difficult patient." If cosmetic surgery guru Mang's prognosis is correct, the little city scooter will be "a hit."
www.merkur-online.de, March 23, 2006

THE NEW DWARF HARDLY BOBS AT ALL

Convertible fun: those who spend an extra 3000 Euros for the cabrio will enjoy their full measure of open-air pleasure. The Smart top can be opened or closed at the push of a button, even at full speed, without any speed restrictions. Not even a Porsche Cabrio can do that.
Aachener Nachrichten, March 14, 2007

DEALERS HOT FOR SMART

Small car maker smart is encountering great interest on the part of American auto dealers, as it builds up a U.S. distribution network prior to market introduction of the new fortwo in the coming year. At the Geneva show, Klaus Maier, the new chief of DaimlerChrysler's smart brand, told Automobilwoche: "Dealer interest is huge. We have about 1400 firm inquiries... Customers in the USA are eagerly anticipating the smart fortwo."
Automobilwoche, March 12, 2007

A LITTLE BIT MORE

In its second incarnation, the Fortwo remains a genuine Smart, without sacrificing any of its charm. The new size is unobtrusive; to the contrary, the two-seater appears noticeably more refined.
Auto/Straßenverkehr, 07.02.2007

BIG SMARTS

The concept is still unique, and so Mercedes is holding on to its city scooter.
ams, 31.01.2007

OUT INTO THE BIG, WIDE WORLD

"The Smart is, as always, revolutionary. It has never been copied. It was a unique concept."
Die Welt, 30.01.2007

The cleanest volume production car on the planet.
Bild, 26.01.2007

"The midget can be guided through curves with greater precision; the new steering reacts precisely. The pitching kiddie car has truly matured into a grown-up small car."
Focus, 13.11.2006

BIGGER IN THE CITY

The ForTwo has grown up! It maintains all of the virtues of the original car, but adds a higher-quality interior, more space and a much-improved driving experience.
Auto Express, January 30, 2007

"Gone are the quirky curves of the original City Coupé, replaced with a more grown-up Mercedes dashboard"
Auto Express, November 15, 2006

A LITTLE BIT SOFTER

[Une dose 'assouplissant]

Except for two-wheelers, there's nothing better in the city.

Action Automoto, 01.03.2007

THE LITTLE ONE HAS GROWN UP

[La petite a bien grandi]

A development which clearly grows out of past success.

Le Moniteur Automobile, 22.02.2007

SMART MOVE

[*Una mossa astuta*]

The interior is bigger and more comfortable, thanks also to the new suspension...and the new seats, with a sportier design, but better contoured and padded.

Auto Oggi, 21.02.2007

The most economical vehicle in the world right now is the new Smart Diesel, with a fuel consumption of about 3.3 liters and 88 g/km CO_2...

Sonntags-Zeitung, 11.03.2007

The Smart has grown up.

Blick, 30.01.2007

HUNTING PARKING SPOTS IN MADRID

The urban environment remains the domain of the smart. A length increase of 19.5 cm does not play any role... In hunting for a parking spot, the smart will always be ahead by a nose, even if we completely disregard its prestige value.

Tiroler Tageszeitung, 17.02.2007

As if that weren't enough, the most eagerly anticipated new production car debuting in Detroit, home of the V8 muscle car, may be the tiny Smart Fortwo, a three-cylinder European minicar you could park in a walk-in closet.

Detroit Free Press, January 7, 2007

I am so convinced of its safety and reliability that I am planning to drive one coast-to-coast in the United States.

Washington Post, January 11, 2007

2

ANALYSIS & PROGNOSIS

smart city coupé, 1998

Willi Diez

2.0 THE FUTURE OF A PROJECT

- or, why the smart brand would have to be invented today, if it didn't already exist

2.1 Introduction

In the contemporary repertoire of clever aphorisms, Mikhail Gorbachev's comment that "He who comes too late is punished by life" resonates so thoroughly in modern society that it would be difficult to advance the converse: that life also punishes those who arrive too early. Yet the histories of politics, culture, and economics are filled with prominent examples to illustrate the point. Walter Rathenau, one of the anticipators of a unified Europe, paid for his vision with his life, and Henri Rousseau, one of the trailblazers of modern art, had to suffer under the label of "Sunday painter" during his own lifetime.

Visionaries and prophets have not always been treated kindly by history. This is just as true in the auto industry as elsewhere. The legendary "Tropfenwagen" (Teardrop Car) of 1921, with a then-sensational cD (drag coefficient) of 0.28, brought its inventor, Edmund Rumpler, neither economic fortune nor personal success. Only a few examples of Rumpler's Tropfenwagen were ever sold, but one stands today as one of the most admired exhibits in Munich's Deutsches Museum. Cars are like people: lack of fame during their own lifetime is often followed by immortality after their passing.

Thanks to early publicity, when the "smart city coupe" was first presented to the public at the 1997 Frankfurt International Auto Show, it already enjoyed a genuine fan following, drawn primarily from the ranks of young, well-educated, urban singles. And, as usual in such cases, there was no shortage of doubters and scoffers who tried to dismiss the whole thing as yet another quirky idea on the part of some wacky auto industry executives and a watchmaker incompetent in the ways of the automobile.

Even in the 1980s, Lothar Späth, then prime minister of the province of Baden-Württemberg, himself known for promoting innovation in the land of tinkerers and inventors, had remarked sarcastically about his fellow citizens that *"When in Germany somebody comes up with a new idea, there are immediately twenty people who will explain to him why it won't work."* And, Späth continued, it should come as no surprise that the spirit of invention lay fallow, and ever fewer innovations were developed and realized.

At its appearance, the smart city coupe captivated the world, but did not conquer it. For a long time, it appeared that the critics would be proven right. The "smart," as it was soon called, didn't seem to catch on, and it appeared that it would fade away even before it could really enter market. A deadline was set, by which date a certain sales goal needed to be reached, or the project would come to an early demise just less than two years after its start. The target – 80,000 units for 1999 – was achieved, marque and enterprise were saved, but, as it turned out, only temporarily.

Life punishes those who arrive too soon – and afterwards, everybody will say "I told you so." The smart nearly became yet another one of those boring stories of a good idea ahead of its time. One could almost see the crocodile tears rolling down the cheeks of derisive critics, when something happened to give the whole affair a dramatic turnaround: global warming! Suddenly, the experts had known it all along: if the smart brand didn't already exist, it would now have to be invented.

2.2 A BRIEF OUTLINE OF SMART HISTORY

Phase I: From brownfield to greenfield– "Not just another car"

One cannot understand the creation of the smart brand, and the decision on the part of Mercedes management to build an innovative city car in cooperation with Swatch inventor Nicolas Hayek, without considering the situation of Daimler-Benz AG in general and in particular the Mercedes-Benz marque in the early 1990s. Even though the project had not actually been laid to rest, it was already obvious that the vision of "Daimler-Benz, the technology company" would not be fulfilled. Contrary to all official rhetoric, hope dwindled of ever making real money in non-automotive fields.

At the same time, the Mercedes-Benz marque was stuck in a deep crisis, and not just an economic one. The financial numbers got worse from year to year, the image was more than a little tarnished, and finally, the then-new S-Class, the W140, derided by cynical competitors as a "cathedral on wheels," prompted the question of whether, from a product planning standpoint, "bigger, faster, more expensive" was really the way to a successful future

BB F 5925

BB AD 401

BB F 5928

BB AF 925

BB S 6016

BB AF 923

BB F 5120

BEST
MUSICAL
SPAMALOT
SPAMALOT
Mike Nichols

BB F 4111

BB F 5120

BB F 1788

BB AF 124

BB F 4468

DO NOT
ENTER
STARBUCKS COFFEE

BB F 5120

Criticism of Mercedes-Benz' model strategy grew, not just in the media and in public, but also internally. Even then, the expression "rehabilitation candidate" made the rounds. Everything was examined: the model lineup, production processes, and, last but not least, the overall marque strategy. The result of this, literally, radical – as in, going to the roots – analysis of the problems was a strategic realignment in product politics: young, emotional models were to conquer new customer groups. "Premium in every class," was the new slogan, under which the "first product offensive" was initiated, resulting in model lines which were as fascinating as they were successful: SLK, CLK, and the M-Class.

During this period of product line upheaval, first thoughts were given to development of an unconventional, innovative small car. In principle, there were two projects, pursued in parallel, and of which no one knew whether one, or both – or neither – of the vehicle concepts would be developed to the point of being ready for production. Along with first thoughts in the direction of Swatch, there was also a project known internally as NFG – for "Neue Fahrzeuggeneration," New Vehicle Generation, which later became the A-Class.

The idea of the Swatchmobile originated with Nicolas Hayek, who desired to transfer to the automobile his philosophy, which he had already implemented so successfully in the watch industry: apply unconventional design, an attractive marketing concept, and, ultimately, an inviting price to an everyday product to bring an appealing lifestyle product to market, one which everyone could afford. Despite hopeful beginnings, talks with various manufacturers, including Volkswagen, ultimately led nowhere.

It was different at Mercedes. There, it was not just a question of a single vehicle, but rather something which to this day is still completely underestimated in any public analysis of the smart project: a determination to leave the beaten path, from development, through production, all the way to distribution. The solution was called "all car would not be a "mini Mercedes" and would not be developed, produced, or distributed as such, but rather it would become a testbed for innovations in development, production, and distribution. So it came as no surprise that a career changer, Helmut Werner (who had come from the tire industry and now served as chairman of the board of Mercedes-Benz AG), together with passenger car director Jürgen Hubbert, served as the most important protagonists of the project, which was long debated internally. On March 4, 1994, a press

[1]

[1] limited/1 special edition (1998) and edition red (2006) first and last models of the first-generation fortwo

conference was called to announce a planned joint venture between Daimler-Benz AG and the manufacturer of Swatch watches, Nicolas Hayek and his company, SMH.

The desire to build something completely new with this car, on a figurative as well as literal "greenfield," explains why the smart was not docked to existing branches within the Mercedes organization, but rather led to the deliberate founding of a separate business, largely independent of the existing organization. There was to be no "Mercedesation," and so its separation from Mercedes became a part of the smart brand and business structure.

This tendency toward independence and innovation in all areas was consistently applied within the framework of the MCC project.

DEVELOPMENT: The smart city coupé was the first car to be consistently developed in modular form. Moreover, the vehicle was equipped with numerous engineering features not commonly found in its class, packaged in a young, fresh design which most definitely did not resemble a Mercedes-Benz. The smart was to have everything expected of a small car, and more, but within compact dimensions; not "reduced to the minimum," but rather "reduced to the max," in the words of the marque's first slogan.

[1]

[2]

PRODUCTION: smart production was organized completely differently from what had been standard practice in the auto industry. Suppliers were integrated in the newly built plant in Hambach, Lorraine, France, and therefore provided a portion of the overall capital investment. The close proximity of suppliers to final assembly resulted in an appreciable reduction in assembly time, benefiting not only productivity but also quality of the product.

DISTRIBUTION: Instead of relying on authorized dealerships, the distribution model instead employed a franchise system, intended to ensure a standardized brand image at the point of sale. Emphasis was to be placed not on the individual dealer, but rather on the brand itself. The "smart towers" became a visible expression of this distribution philosophy; these no longer bore any relationship to the traditional auto dealership concept.

But smart not only sought to revolutionize the automobile: *"Not just another car,"* in the words of the announcement, signaling that the new two-seat minicar was also intended to realize a new vision for mobility in the 21st century – the vision of a mobility concept that transcended the vehicle itself, and was tailored to traffic problems in urban centers. According to an early programmatic exposition of the concept's goals, *"Smart is on the one hand an ultra-compact city coupe, and, on the other, a completely new urban mobility concept, composed of a multitude of additional products and services intended to make individual city transportation more efficient, more human, and more rational."* The intention was to offer, under the trade name "smartmove," various mobility services, such as special car rental discounts for those occasions when a larger vehicle was needed, special parking management in cities, and combined utilization of automobile and rail transport.

[3]

The revolutionary impetus that marked the beginning of this project may, in retrospect, appear strangely removed from reality. But this was carried by genuine concern for the future of the automobile in an increasingly auto-critical world: *"If we want to continue living as we have,"* declared Johann Tomforde, the spiritual father of the smart, on the occasion of the city coupe's world premiere at the 1997 Frankfurt Auto Show, *"we must bid farewell to exaggerated status symbols, and turn toward new values. In urban areas, vehicle external size and top speed will lose their prestige value. The demands for safety and operating comfort, environmental responsibility, agility and maneuverability will increase. Our smart is convincing proof that with our individualistic, characteristic city coupe, we are on the right path."*

smart Center
[1] Service area
[2] Showroom
[3] External appearance with smart tower

[1]

[2]

Phase II: From mobility concept to lifestyle product – "Cheap & chic."

When the vehicle finally hit the streets in 1998 – or, better said, was scheduled to hit the streets – the company had other problems on its hands. The A-Class had just flipped over in a so-called "moose test," which only encouraged other test pilots to examine the stability of the smart under a microscope. The result was that in short order, photographs of a smart, with its backside planted firmly on the ground, made the rounds. The problem was quickly eliminated, but the image of the new product had already suffered.

Whether this was the cause, or the vehicle's unconventional appearance, sales of the smart city coupe fell far short of expectations. After 20,000 units had been sold in 1998, the following year saw smart meet its target of 80,000 cars. Yet this was still far removed from the originally planned, and still publicly announced, sales goal.

Perhaps Mercedes boss Jürgen Hubbert was right when he said that if Nicolas Hayek had not communicated a target of 200,000 units, the actual number of 80,000 in the first full year of production would have been celebrated as a grand success for a completely new vehicle concept. Now, however, that number, 200,000, was the elephant in the room, and both the brand and its management were measured against this benchmark.

In the intervening years since the project's initial stages, time and potential customers' value expectations have transformed the original concept into an innovative and unconventional city car. If the early 1990s were still marked by an intense, public debate about the consequences of unchecked growth of motorized personal transportation, a discussion which even the spread of standard three-way catalytic converters could not silence, then the spirit of the second half of the decade was no longer defined by ecological Cassandras and prophets of the apocalypse, but rather by experience-seeking hedonists.

The Internet bubble, the burgeoning economy, and the easy money to be made on the stock market defined the spirit of the country. Topics like ecology and fuel economy were pushed to the background, not least because gasoline and diesel prices rose only gradually. The leap from an ecologically minded to a fun-loving society was also reflected in the public's automotive desires: instead of eco-cars, sport utility vehicles and compact roadsters developed into the fastest-growing market segments. Automobiles which only a few years earlier had been considered "politically incorrect," were now trendsetters. The smart was threatened with banishment to the ecological sidelines; brand repositioning was urgently required.

Without ever really playing a perceptible public role, the vision of an innovative urban mobility concept was quietly buried, and the marketing message converted to one of driving fun and lifestyle. At the end of 1999, a Europe-wide advertising campaign was launched, positioning the smart as an active-driving fun car: "The first affordable Formula One gearshift," was the claim which, among other things, was intended to place the vehicle's pricing in context for many potential customers. Market introduction of the smart cabrio in March 2000 also fit into this strategy.

With this combination of lifestyle and attractive pricing, the smart jumped onto a trend that, in the late 1990s, could be discerned in many consumer goods of the time, summarized in the words "cheap and chic." This trend was and is at right angles to that trend which marketing textbooks label „loss of the center." Loss of the center is intended to mean a disproportionately increasing demand, on one hand, for high-quality and expensive brands and products, on the other hand however a simultaneous demand for cheap, usually disposable goods. The losers in such a scenario are vendors in the middle price and quality range, who are abandoned by customers.

Plausibility of this development is so obvious that it has hidden from view a phenomenon which first gained importance in the garment sector, namely, the success of brands offering fashionable clothes at moderate prices, after the motto "Designed like Prada, priced like Aldi." Brands such as Hennes & Mauritz, Zara, and others positioned themselves in the market with the message: why does anything that's affordable also have to look bad? Beyond familiar Italian, French, and North American exclusive brands with their exorbitant pricing, and far removed from no-name products of department stores and discount chains, in the 1990s the clothing industry saw the establishment of a market segment that combined cheap and chic in an intelligent manner, attractive to young consumers. Cheap and chic was also a motto with which clever smart drivers, and, above all, female drivers, could identify.

In just two years – 1999 and 2000 – the smart city coupe turned into a lifestyle, indeed into a cult product. By way of the mobility concept, the smart finally found its link to the current, relevant social trends of the late 20th century – hedonism, fun, and lifestyle. In the year 2000, sales finally exceeded 100,000 units, a vital benchmark for the marque's survival. Compared to the fantasized 200,000 units, expectations were more in line with reality. But this success formed the foundation of a new ambition.

Phase III: From niche player to full-line manufacturer – "Open your mind"

Just as the vehicle itself was unconventional, so was its life cycle. As a rule, sales of a new model typically peak in the third year, but the smart city coupe sales numbers rose, year after year. However, in a time which places a premium on "shareholder value," one not inconsiderable problem was the fact that smart was not making any money, and the transition to profitability announced for 2004 was clearly not going to happen. The crossblade and, above all, the smart roadster, both introduced for 2002, underscored the brand's youthful, sporty direction, but it was obvious that both models, by the very nature of their concepts, were going to remain absolute niche products.
To become profitable, sales needed to be increased. But this could only be achieved with additional models. On the other hand, there was a Catch-22: expansion of the model line required additional investment for product development and increased production capacity.

To keep these investments as small as possible, it was decided to cooperate with Mitsubishi, which had entered into a strategic alliance with DaimlerChrysler in 2001. The resulting jointly developed product was the smart forfour, called the new Colt at Mitsubishi. In parallel, development was begun on a small sport utility vehicle, announced for 2006 as the smart formore.

This phase also saw a revamping of the brand identity: a new logo, and a new slogan ("open your mind") were intended to convey a sense of departure, of getting underway. The smart organization was expanded, and equipped with the full complement of personnel expected of an auto manufacturer. The results were, initially, even greater financial losses, which had nothing to do with mismanagement but rather with the fact that large investments for the future were not being offset by any short-term returns.

[1] The smart idea as a mobility concept: press conference in Sarreguemines, May 17, 1995
[2] smart as an element of lifestyle culture: press conference in Stuttgart, November 9, 2006

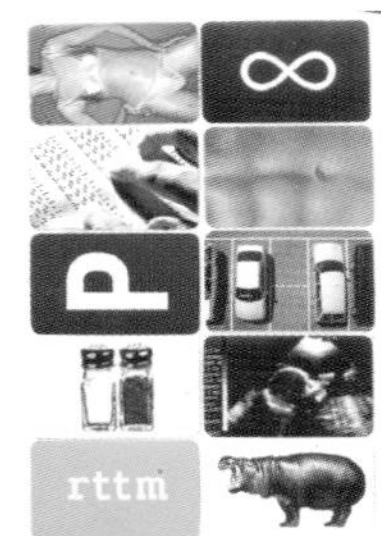

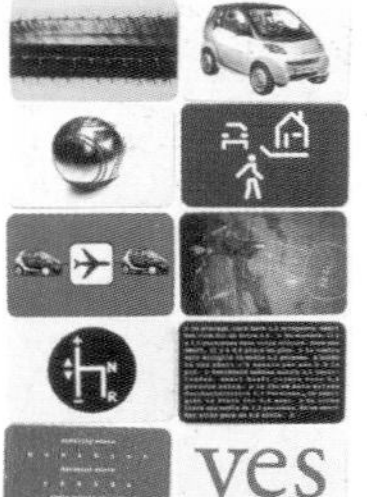

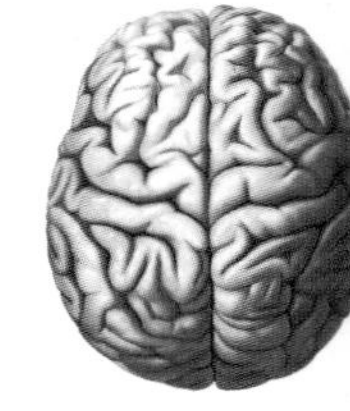

reduce to the max.

reduce to the max.

A picture of the brand comes into focus:
selected print ads and communications efforts, 1997 – 2007.

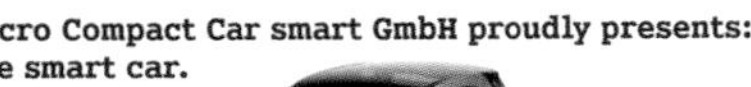

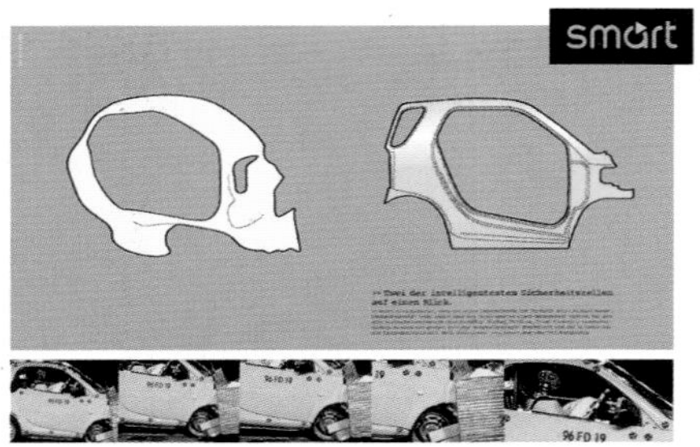

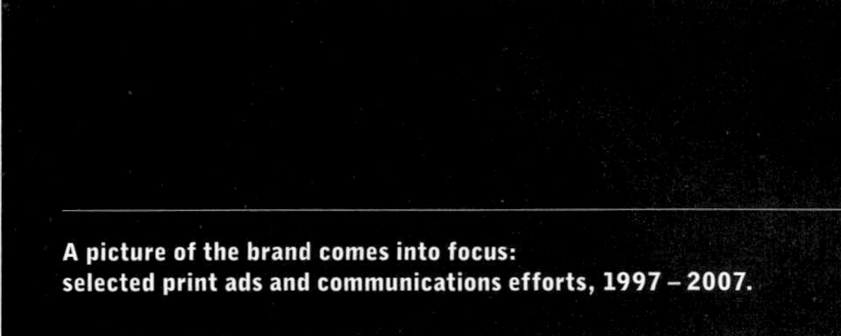

A picture of the brand comes into focus:
selected print ads and communications efforts, 1997 – 2007.

smart
>> Starten
>> Parken

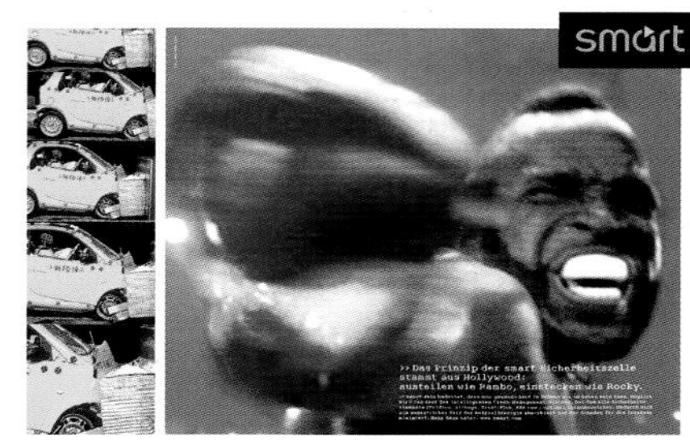
smart

Fabriquee en France.
smart

smart

smart
(SPASS)² =
N
R

smart
>> Hamburgamsterdambrüssel.
Der neue smart: Über 700 km ohne Tankstop.

smart
>> Nizzaflorenzrom.
Der neue smart: Über 700 km ohne Tankstop.

smart
>> Berneflorencevenice.

smart
>> Munichmilannice.

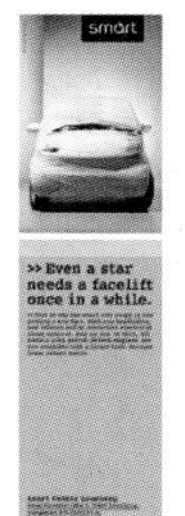
smart
>> Even a star needs a facelift once in a while.

smart

smart

smart

smart

smart

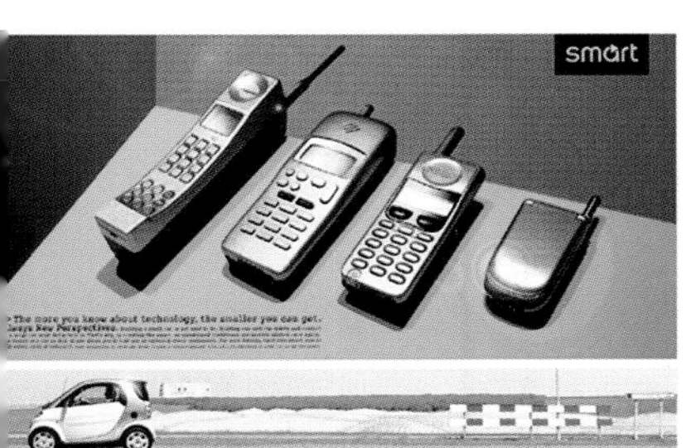
smart

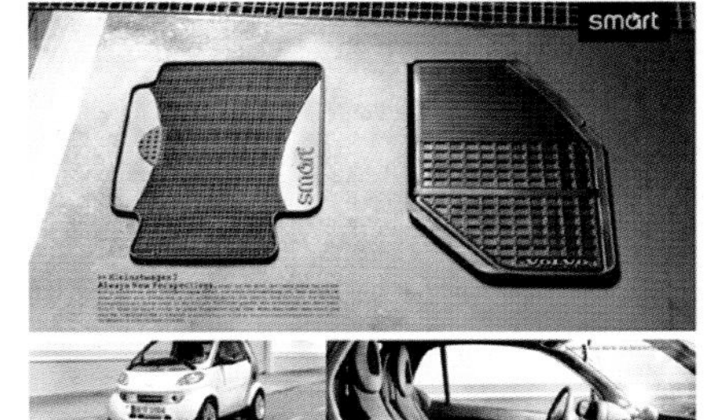
smart

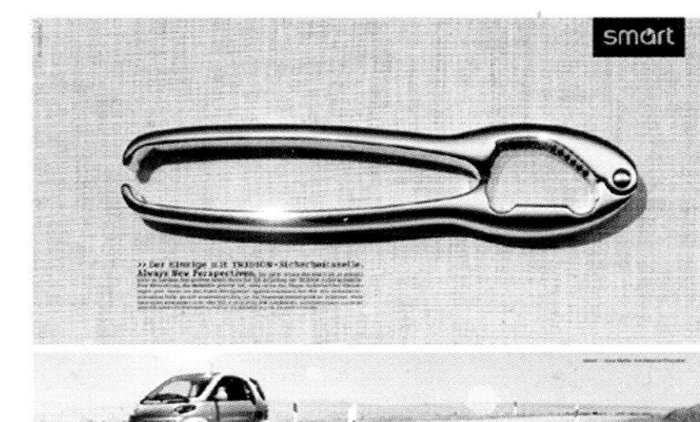
smart

smart

smart

smart
>> Faster through the city.

smart
7654

smart

smart
>> The perfect fit.

smart
open your mind.
B AK 2389

smart
On the 9th of October 2001 smart arrives in Sweden.

smart
THANK YOU FOR ENTERTAINING ME.
THE NEW

smart
open your mind.
I'M A QUICK AND MEAN SHOPPING MACHINE.
I SEE, I P, I CONQUER.
THE NEW

smart
open your mind.
THE NEW

CANARIAS
Fraternidad
PALACE H

But what proved fatal was that even the first of the new model lines, which had been hoped to generate a massive jump in total sales, once again fell far short of overly ambitious targets. The smart forfour, introduced to the market in the spring of 2004, was a flop. Just over 70,000 units were sold in 2004. The market showed its utter disregard for platform strategies or joint production with Mitsubishi; there was no money to be made with this model.

The reasons for failure of the smart forfour are many. Of course, the forfour lacked the originality and differentiation exhibited by the fortwo. Naturally, there were features that allowed it to stand out from its competitors. But the smart forfour was placed in a market segment characterized by gradual decline and ruinous price wars. On price, the forfour could not compete with the mass-market contenders. As a result, a new strategic direction for smart became unavoidable.

Phase IV: And back again: "Back to the Roots"

One could spend a lot of time speculating what might have become of the smart brand if other dark clouds had not been gathering over DaimlerChrysler just as smart's own problems intensified. Perhaps, with typical Swabian thoroughness, the planned strategy would have been pulled off somehow. Or perhaps, if the overall corporate situation had been more positive, one might have settled on a strategy of consolidation.

In any case, between 2001 and 2006, DaimlerChrysler endured turbulent years, not exactly swimming in success. After overcoming Chrysler's first drop in sales and earnings in 2001, Mitsubishi issued a string of negative reports. In early summer of 2004, ties to Mitsubishi were loosened, and, subsequently, DaimlerChrysler's interest in Hyundai was sold off. Shortly thereafter, sales and earnings prospects at the core brand, Mercedes-Benz, began to dim, which led to massive job cuts in 2006.

There was always a crisis somewhere, and it would have taken a very strong commitment to the smart marque to continue on the announced expansion course. The foreseeable expenditures were too high, and the possible sales and earnings increases too uncertain. The consequences were obvious: in front of a backdrop of continuing bad sales figures, in March of 2005 the DaimlerChrysler AG board decided on a restructuring program for the smart brand, whose list of bad news was as long as it was unavoidable. At its core, the solution was called "Back to roots:" smart would once again be a single-product marque, with a new smart fortwo as the vessel for all of the brand's hopes and the engine of its growth. About 1000 jobs were eliminated, all relevant functions integrated in the Mercedes-Benz division, and smart GmbH dissolved as of June 30, 2006.

The second generation of the smart fortwo was presented to the international media on November 9, 2006. Although to the untrained observer, it was hardly distinguishable from its predecessor, the car's engineering and equipment had undergone careful development. The new smart generation was hailed by the media as an advance over the original smart. With that, it appeared that normal everyday operations had returned to a marque that, in the previous few years, had generated headlines and sensation like no other brand.

And so we arrive in the present – reason enough for a small accounting, which could just as easily have turned into a final accounting, but instead is an intermediate summation of an ambitious project which has weathered good times and bad. What has DaimlerChrysler gained by enriching the automotive world with a completely new marque?

[1]

[1] All smart models, on a Danish beach

BE·524813

2.3 AN ACCOUNTING AFTER NINE YEARS – "LESSONS LEARNED"

In the early 1960s, as America's plans for the conquest of space began to consume ever greater sums of money, an increasingly restless public asked what the American citizen had gained from all of these projects. NASA, the national space agency, replied: the Teflon-coated frying pan. Indeed, Teflon was a spinoff from space technology, but this answer was insufficient to dispel the public's reservations about the immense sums consumed by expensive space programs; was it really necessary to launch rockets and people into space in order to keep the ordinary citizen's fried eggs from sticking to the pan?

"smart thinking" – a microcar as an innovation carrier

In smart thinking... the little car that made it big, his highly readable affirmation of love for the smart, author Tony Lewin recounts a meeting of the smart project's first management generation in 2004, on the occasion of the tenth anniversary of the signing of the joint effort agreement between Mercedes-Benz and Swatch: "Looking back over those few years of intense creativity, the reunited smart pioneers realized the scale of their achievement: they counted ten clear industry firsts, ranging from the module-based manufacturing concept and the integration of suppliers as system partners to the tridion safety cell, the innovative powertrain and the now-distinctive smart-tower dealer concept."

Indeed, even the most vocal critics of the project did not dispute the fact that many of the advances first realized by smart have now become state of the art in the auto industry. All of the world's auto manufacturers have profited from the once-young auto marque's willingness to experiment.

But what of DaimlerChrysler? How do its balance sheets look? Have the results justified the huge effort expended? On the positive side of the ledger are three items which are difficult to evaluate from a monetary standpoint:

- smart is a strong, well-known brand
- smart has given a positive impulse to the corporate culture, and, finally,
- smart has won new customers and friends for the company as a whole.

On the negative side, of course, are the years of losses piled up by smart, the consequences of a business model which was not modified in time. As right as it might have been in the early stages to give smart its own life and every creative opportunity necessary for realizing fundamental innovations, so it was a fatal error to hold on to the entrepreneurial independence of smart when it became obvious that planned sales targets would not be met. Rather than continuing to inflate the operation's head count, it would have made more sense to make timely use of synergies with the Mercedes-Benz marque. Instead, smart ran headlong into a money pit, from which it could only be freed by a painful jolt.

It would be presumptuous to suggest that DaimlerChrysler would be a completely different company today if it hadn't been for smart. But it is beyond dispute that smart not only became a sympathetic icon for the company, but also credible evidence for the concern's willingness to innovate. smart polarizes, but what better can be said of a marque that seeks to be noticed, and taken seriously.

The revolution devours its own children: what remains of the Swatchmobile

By the time Nicolas Hayek, initiator and inspiration of the entire project, gave up his shares of the Micro Compact Car (MCC) joint venture on November 1, 1998, his vision of a vehicle fitted with alternative propulsion was already history. With his Swatchmobile, Hayek wanted to do more than just build a small car; he wanted to launch a new age of mobility, and to that end, he felt it was necessary that the smart be offered with electric and hybrid propulsion. Indeed, company documents from the early days show that alternative propulsion systems were always under discussion; in the course of the model's life cycle, these were to be rounded out by gasoline and diesel powerplants.

In view of the current euphoria for hybrid drives and a reawakened interest in electric cars, one might be tempted to speak of missed opportunities with the early smart. If smart had become the first volume-production car on the market with hybrid drive, would the crowned leader in terms of environmental responsibility be DaimlerChrysler instead of Toyota? On the other hand, completely aside from any questions of whether they made engineering sense, the question arises of whether smart could have weathered the financial cost of developing alternative propulsion systems.

Perhaps it is this which Jürgen Hubbert meant with his comment on Nicolas Hayek's role, when he said, *"Without Nicolas Hayek, there would be no smart. But it wouldn't exist with him, either."*

Hayek interpreted the development of the smart project as a betrayal of his ideas, and made no secret of his feelings in many public statements. Even today, he continues to seek an industrial partner who will work with him to realize the dream of a revolutionary small car. And who could hold it against him?

Nothing succeeds like success

When Neil Armstrong became the first man to step onto the Moon on July 21, 1969, nobody in the USA asked how much the Apollo 11 mission had cost. Pride and joy ruled the land on that day. "One small step for a man, one giant leap for mankind" – and America celebrated.

Five prototypes with five different propulsion systems: left to right, microhybrid, diesel full hybrid, electric drive, CNG (compressed natural gas), and CDI (common rail diesel injection).

The smart fortwo i-move edition anticipated a trend. Limited to 150 examples, the special edition was sold out within days. For the first time, a car manufacturer provided an integrated Apple iPod. (Geneva, 2004).

1/min
x1000

2.4 QUO VADIS SMART?

Climate change – the beginning of a new automotive age?

Quite possibly, February 2, 2007 will go down in history as a turning point in the development of motorized individual transport. The report by the United Nations Intergovernmental Panel on Climate Change unleashed worldwide consternation and anxiety, comparable in its effect to the 1972 study by a team of MIT researchers, The Limits to Growth. The UN report's conclusions, that global temperatures could rise by as much as 6.4 °C (11.5 °F) by the end of the 21st century, and that this is caused by human activities, are conclusions which call forth not only a willingness, but also an urgency to deal with the problem. Naturally, history has given a lie to many a prognostication. Today, however, in the face of broad scientific consensus, few will argue with the prognosis of a rising, grave greenhouse effect which can only be countered by immediate, vigorous action.

[2]

[1]

Over the next years and decades, we will be confronted by the consequences of climate change, perhaps not every day, but time and again. Warmer winters, storms, and other natural catastrophes, or the gradual melting of the polar ice caps – climate change will shape the news we see in our media. It would be very strange indeed if, sooner or later, this did not influence human attitudes and behavior. Nobody wants to forego individual mobility, but voiced or not, the question of sustainability of one's own behavior has to be on the agenda of anyone shopping for an automobile.

If nothing else, politics will see to it – after, as usual, first plunging headlong into senseless action for its own sake in order to telegraph to the concerned citizenry a willingness to take action. In the long term, there will be development of an overall environmental and energy policy whose goal must be to minimize CO_2 emissions in a meaningful, lasting manner. Introduction of a European Union automotive CO_2 limit of 130 g/km by 2012 represents only the beginning of further political initiatives, on both national and international levels.

It is indeed moving to read the following, from an analysis of the market possibilities of a small, two-seat city car from the year 1996:

- "Intensification of the global environmental problem sensitizes and emotionalizes a continually growing environmental awareness"
- "The rising cost of mobility due to dwindling energy resources causes an appreciable increase in ecological and economical demands placed on a modern personal vehicle"

and finally

- "Introduction of a CO_2 / energy tax"

Today, the automotive scenario for the coming years and decades could not be described any differently – even if there are intervening periods of dropping oil prices and calming fears of impending ecological meltdown. When it comes to awareness of problems, humans have at best a short attention span. But ecological challenges will repeatedly catch up to the apparently unstoppable march of humanity, and, it is to be feared, do so with growing intensity.

The smart fortwo, long relegated to the shadow if its bigger brother, suddenly shines forth with the lowest CO_2 emissions of any vehicle offered in Europe. But glowing reviews are no guarantee for

commercial success, and many a leader in renowned rankings has, in the end, gone home empty-handed.

LOHAS – a car finds its target group

A clever automotive manager once declared that one did not build cars for politicians, but rather for customers. That may sound arrogant, but hits the problem on the head. For often, what political decision makers want – the reasonable, functional, and environmentally responsible automobile – is not what the customers want, or at least not a sufficiently large number of them. The history of ecomobiles is a history of marketplace flops, and it is of little benefit to the environment if ultra-ecological cars are displayed at auto shows, praised by politicians, but rejected by customers.

At the beginning of this decade, sociologist Paul H. Ray and psychologist Sherry Ruth Anderson discovered a new consumer group in American society. They claim that 30 percent of all American consumers belong to this group. After Yuppies, DINKs ("double income, no kids") and BOBOs ("Bourgeoise Bohemians"), they call this group LOHAS: "Lifestyles of Health and Sustainability."

The LOHAS movement even has its own web site, on which we read: "LOHAS is... a market segment focused on health and fitness, the environment, personal development, sustainable living, and social justice." Elsewhere we read *"... New values, new awareness, human needs directed inward, a lifestyle reversal to self-realization, stress reduction, decompression, health, sustainability and durability. All of this translates into a demand for healthy, economically and ecologically sensible products and services."*

Despite their doubtless ecological orientation, LOHAS do not see themselves as anti-consumers. *"They are by no means opposed to new technologies, although it is important to them that innovations bring a personal benefit, and are in harmony with their ecological awareness."* Accordingly, this rapidly growing consumer segment represents *"a potentially huge market in the following segments: ecological products such as organically-grown food, or in the fashion segment with textiles, home construction, interior decoration, alternative energy, 'green money,' ecotourism as well as alternative energy sources and ecologically responsible, sensibly produced and operated vehicles."*

LOHAS are a generation of consumers who are aware of the limited, finite nature of our natural resources, and for whom such products are attractive which not only protect the environment, but also soothe their own consciences. They would like to feel good about having a good time.

Somewhere between Greens in bib overalls and blatant materialists, the first stereotypes are forming: good-looking thirtysomethings who dearly love their Burberry cashmere scarf, but pay close attention to ensure that "fair trade" rules are observed. Or the slightly graying 40-year-old in a Ralph Lauren Polo shirt, living in an energy-efficient home of steel, concrete, and glass, enjoying his organically raised lamb chop with a Chilean Cabernet Sauvignon.

Left page
[1] World Solar Challenge in Australia, 2005
[2] The new smart fortwo CDI has the lowest CO_2 emissions of any automobile

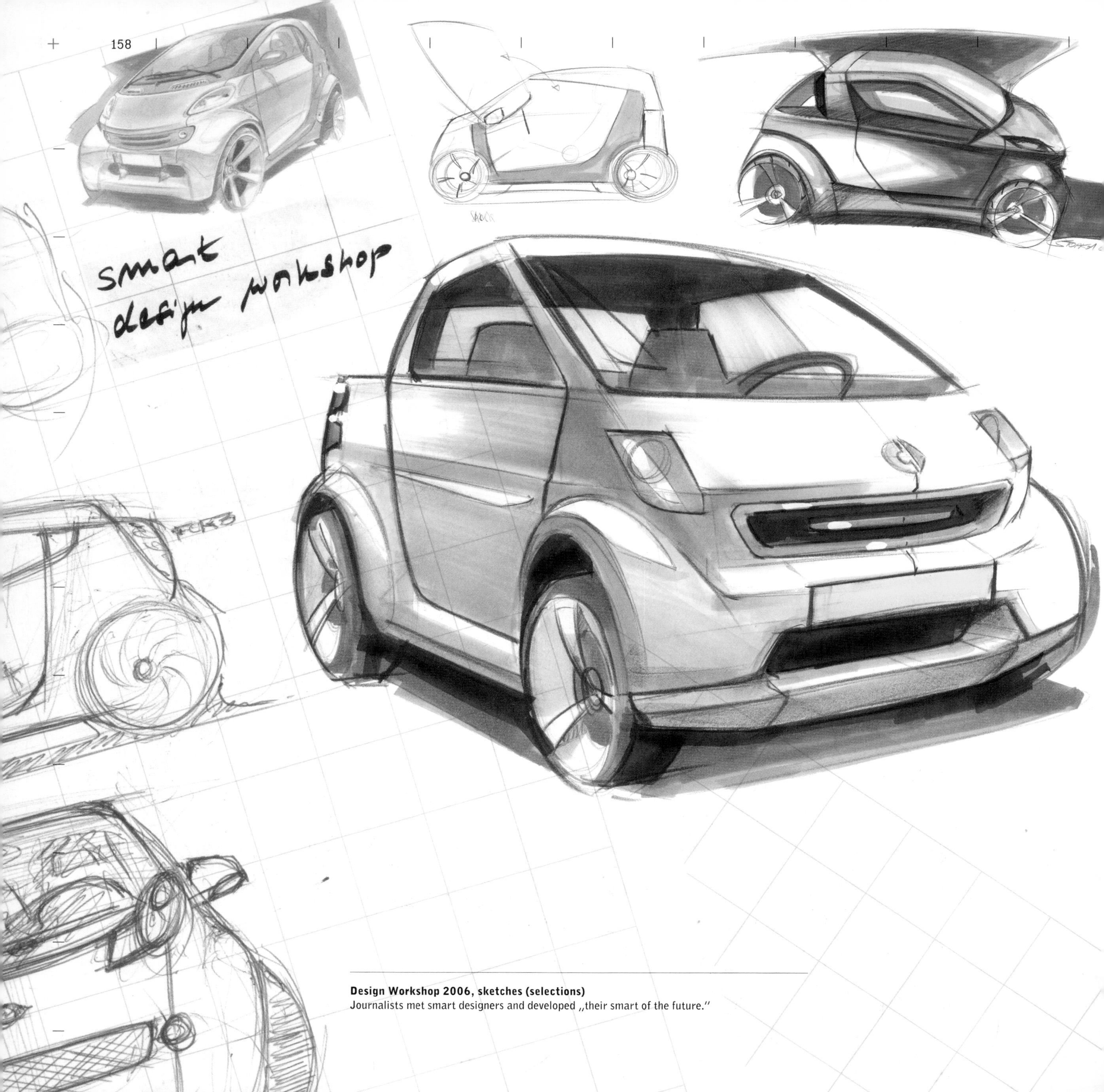

Design Workshop 2006, sketches (selections)
Journalists met smart designers and developed ,,their smart of the future."

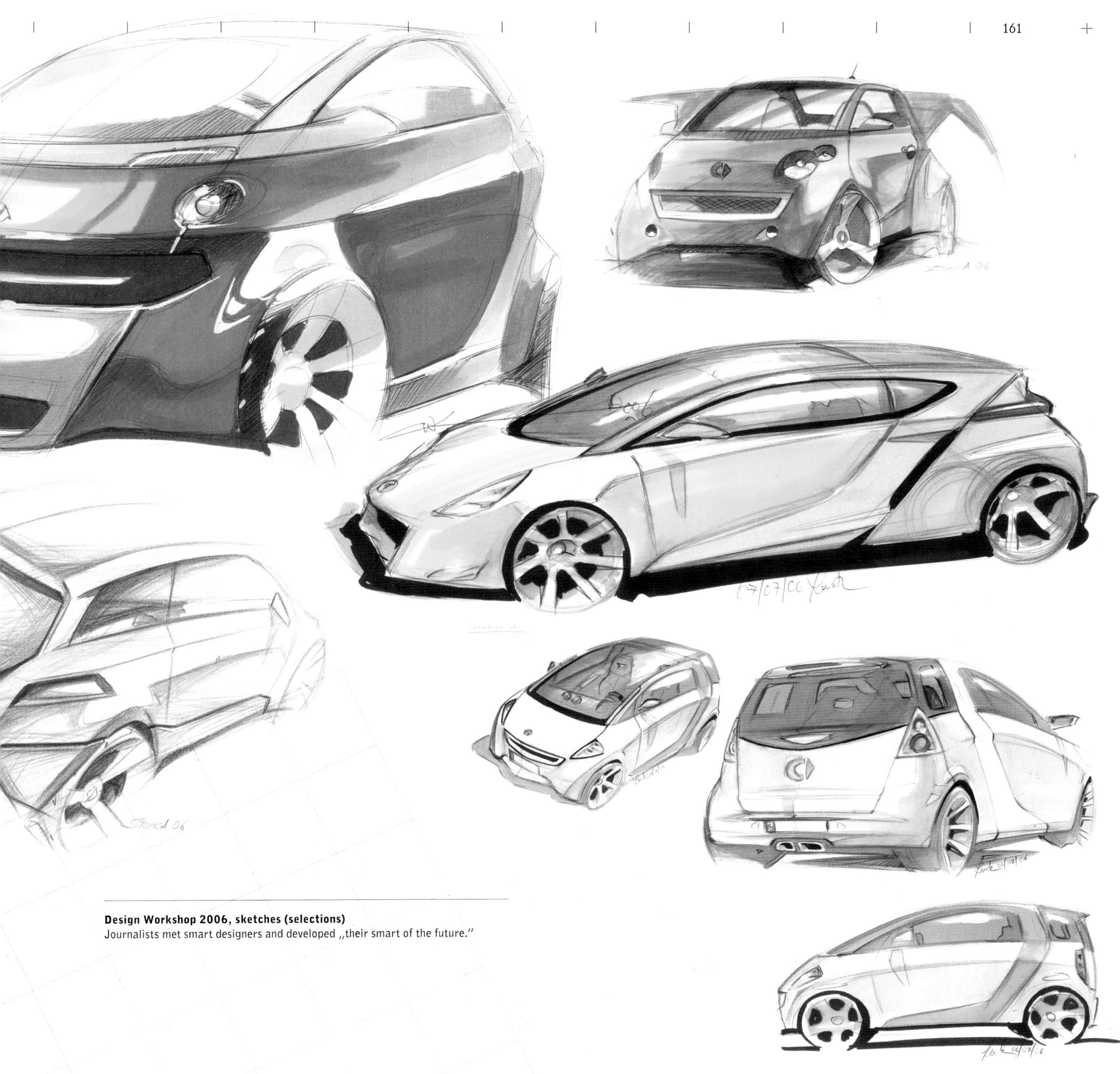

Design Workshop 2006, sketches (selections)
Journalists met smart designers and developed „their smart of the future."

The smart fortwo is an outstanding example of the fact that the image of a brand or product is not solely shaped by its manufacturer, but also by its typical customers. Precisely the fortwo has gradually conquered a customer base which may be described by adjectives such as youthful, urban, extroverted, ecology-minded, and brand aware. Those who want to be noticed can, of course, always achieve that with an especially expensive and luxurious car. But that can also be done with a smart fortwo, and, in keeping with the motto *"I don't need that,"* in an understated way that comes off as personable rather than pretentious.

In a description of the smart fortwo target group, dated 1998, we read *"The smart target group shares the view that economically and ecologically sensible behavior in urban traffic cannot be achieved for free. Intellectually, this group is above average, and will make the smart into a symbol of intelligence, which in turn will force the hand of a completely different group of people."* The smart target group has arrived in the present, in the guise of the LOHAS.

2.5 SMARTISM – IN PRAISE OF PERSISTENCE

In his book *Anders ist besser* ("Different is Better"), Porsche CEO Wendelin Wiedeking lambastes the short-term mindset which has infected many companies under the pressure of flinty-eyed analysts. Porsche's success, according to Wiedeking, is proof that an organization can only enjoy continuous success if it thinks beyond day-to-day, or better said quarterly, profits, and acts accordingly; "Our business is of a long-term nature. Anybody who builds cars needs to breathe deeply."

Imagine if the board of DaimlerChrysler AG had decided, in the spring of 2006, to close down the smart brand, and abandon the manufacture of small cars. The stock market would have celebrated, and today, as BMW sells its Mini and Audi is about to launch a small car, DaimlerChrysler would be left without the very model which has rightfully and repeatedly been awarded the "Environmental Certificate" of the Öko-Trend environmental research institute. The smart fortwo will not solve the problem of global warming. But it is an important contribution to any eventual solution. And, in the future, all manufacturers will need such products in their lines, if they want to survive in the global marketplace.

The logic of capital markets is not a logic of industrial sustainability; sometimes persistence does have its rewards. A financial portfolio can change daily, but the product portfolio of an auto manufacturer can change only on time scales of 5 to 15 years. In these very times, whether we like it or not, the future scenario of the automobile has changed. Those who have neglected to add global warming to their agenda will face difficult times in the markets of the future. Mikhail Gorbachov was right: *"He who comes too late is punished by life."*

[1]

[1] A handshake for a smart future in the USA: Dieter Zetsche and Roger Penske, Detroit, June 28, 2006

[4]

[5]

[6]

[10]

[11]

[12]

from upper left to lower right:
[1] eco sprinter (1993) **[2]** eco speedster (1993) **[3]** eco speedster interior (1993) **[4]** Atlanta show car (1996) **[5]** Paris show car (1996) **[6]** smart city coupé fashion victim (1997) **[7]** DaimlerChrysler plant fire brigade (1998) **[8]** smart professional interior (1999) **[9]** smart professional (1999) **[10]** smart cabrio (2000) **[11]** smart transparent (2000) **[12]** smart cabrio Right Hand Drive (2001) **[13]** smart crossblade show car (2001) **[14]** smart BRABUS fortwo (2002) **[15]** smart BRABUS fortwo cabrio (2002) **[16]** smart crosstown show car (2005)

[16]

2007: SMART FORTWO II

Ten years after the first preproduction smarts rolled off the assembly line, the new smart fortwo enters the marketplace. The engineers have built on the strengths of this visionary classic, and refined the marque's virtues. The new smart fortwo fascinates customers in its established markets. And, for the first time, it will carry the smart idea to the American market.

2007

SMART FORTWO II

The new smart fortwo, 2006

smart fortwo coupé

smart fortwo cabrio

smart fortwo coupé

Nordwest Richt. Rheinweg
20:08
Menü
250
20
30
40
50
60
80
100
120
140
160
1
2
LOAD
ON
BASS TREB
BAL FADE
MENU

smart
BB F 2231

smart fortwo cabrio

smart
BB F 4231

smart fortwo limited one

BB F 4222

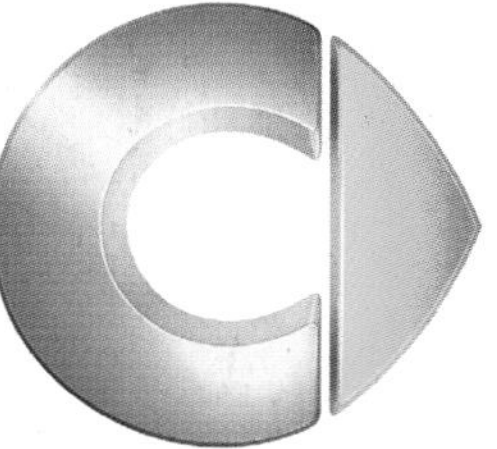